Who Put the Cat in the Fridge?

serving up hope and hilarity family style

D1295593

Who Put the Cat in the Fridge?

serving up hope and hilarity family style

Rhonda Rhea

LIFE JOURNEY®

Bringing Home the Message for Life

COOK COMMUNICATIONS MINISTRIES
Colorado Springs, Colorado • Paris, Ontario
KINGSWAY COMMUNICATIONS LTD
Eastbourne, England

Life Journey® is an imprint of
Cook Communications Ministries, Colorado Springs, Colorado 80918
Cook Communications, Paris, Ontario
Kingsway Communications, Eastbourne, England

WHO PUT THE CAT IN THE FRIDGE?
© 2005 by Rhonda Rhea

Cover Design & Photo: TrueBlue Design/Sandy Flewelling

First Printing, 2005
Printed in the United States of America
1 2 3 4 5 6 7 8 9 10 Printing/Year 08 07 06 05

Library of Congress Cataloging-in-Publication Data

Rhea, Rhonda.
  Who put the cat in the fridge? / Rhonda Rhea.
    p. cm.
  Includes bibliographical references (p.   ).
  ISBN 0-7814-4190-0 (pbk.)
  1. Family--Religious life. 2. Christian life. I. Title.
BV4526.3.R44 2005
248.4--dc22
                                    2004024896

• • • • •

One more time, mega love and thanks to my family. To Richie, my wonderful, kind, loving friend and hubby. What would I do without you? Thank you so much for your support, encouragement, and inspiration.

And to my five most favorite kids in all the world: Andrew, Jordan, Kaley, Allie, and Daniel. The encouragement you provide is such a blessing. The material you provide is such a hoot.

contents

• • • • •

Part 1: Rip-roaring Recipes for Fast-moving Fun—Relying on Christ in the Adventure

Part 2: A Dash of This, a Dash of That—Dealing with the Busyness of Life

Part 3: Blending Together Thoroughly—Keeping Christ at the Center of Every Relationship

Part 4: Sticking to the Recipe, Tasting Sweet Results—Disciplining and Instructing

Part 5: If at First You Don't Succeed, Fry, Fry Again—Persevering through the Challenging Moments

Part 6: Stirring Up a Big Batch of Belief—Building Family Faith

Part 7: What Are You Serving?—Serving and Teaching the Family to Serve

Part 8: Love-covered Hearts with Happy-cream Filling—Loving Wholeheartedly

introduction

• • • • •

If You Can't Stand the Heat,
Stop Setting the Kitchen on Fire

Is there a recipe for cooking up a happy family life? Does family life come with directions? We get a manual the size of the Chicago phone book to put together a bicycle, but we're allowed to get married and even take little people home from the hospital (as long as we give birth to them) without so much as a permit. Where's the home manual for, well, the *home*?

Whew! What a relief to know that God gave us the Family Action Manual for Instruction in Leading Youths to Bible-truths (F.A.M.I.L.Y. Bible). He gave us his Word, and he included everything we need to achieve successful family life from birth to Glory.

You know what would really be crazy? Having the recipe and still trying to cook something up on my own (and I don't have a great track record even with the cookbook). Or—even crazier—having the family instruction manual and never reading it! I watched my husband put together a bicycle that came with instructions in every language but ours. It did not go very *bien* or *güt*, but it finally did go together. It went together the hard way. And there were parts left over. I hope that doesn't come back to haunt us.

Families are eternally more important than main dishes or bicycles. Sadly, it's so easy to give more attention to learning how to put together the perfect lasagna or the perfect bike, but neglect investing time studying how the perfect Savior can lead us to put our families together in just the right way. Isn't it exasperating to spend hours learning how to work the DVD player—and more hours figuring out how to get our computers to spit out the right information? Or to spend endless hours getting kids to and from soccer practice, music lessons, orthodontist appointments, and all the other activities that fill their days? Wouldn't it be heartbreaking if we spent most of our time on those things of smaller importance, yet little or no time on the instructions regarding the biggest project of all: the spiritual feeding and well-being of our families?

My family loves fried ravioli. A few years back, I decided to cook up a big batch. I put a pan on the back burner and a glass plate on the front burner. Then I put a towel on the plate to get it all ready for the ravioli. Want to know what I did next? I turned on the burner. Logical move. But I accidentally turned on the front burner instead of the back one. I was doing something at the sink when, WHAMMO! The plate exploded! The towel shot up, then landed on the burner, and poofed into a little fireball. I grabbed the tongs and snatched up the baby fireball, but I didn't make it very far before it fell to the floor. Did I mention I had carpet in my kitchen? Suddenly I was doing an Indian rain-type dance to put out my carpet—it was just this side of "stop, drop, and roll." As I danced, I was already planning my embarrassment over how this story was going to look on the insurance claim form. *Maybe a small throw rug would look nice.*

Who Put the Cat in the Fridge? is a hefty helping of family-style grace served up to provide a good stop, drop, and roll-on-the-floor laugh, and then encouragement to dip into the Manual for the instructions we need to keep our families functioning, fruitful, and fireball-free. A hearty laugh is good for us—especially when it's combined with a beefy helping of God's Word.

Second Timothy 3:16–17 tells us that Scripture is God-breathed and has multi-fruitful uses in our lives. We're told in verse 17 that it's God's Word that will help us become "thoroughly equipped for every good work."

God's Word is something we never want to leave on the back burner. It's the Manual that equips us in even the most strenuous bicycle-building moments and helps us make every part of family life a good work. For all those who are rolling their eyes over the humongous challenges of family life, or for those who would just like a good, endorphin-inducing chuckle connected to a spiritual charge, this book will provide just what you need to keep going. We can laugh and learn as the heart message takes the focus straight to the source of real joy, real direction, real spiritual nourishment—the kind we can only find in Christ.

My hope is that as you read this book, you will relate to a few familiar family happenings with a chuckle or two along the way. With lots of Scripture tucked inside, many of the chapters could be read as fun family devotions on busy days. It's also my hope that every chapter will be an inspiration to dig even more deeply into the Manual. You'll never have to worry about having parts leftover! I'm also happy to report that there's nothing you'll find in God's Manual that will ever require a throw rug.

Get ready to **STOP** the busyness for a minute or two, **DROP** to your knees when the Lord calls you to, and **ROLL** on the floor laughing when you need to!

part one

Rip-roaring Recipes for Fast-moving Fun

Relying on Christ in the Adventure

chapter one

Watch Me!

"Watch me, Mom!" That's kid language. When translated into parent language, it means, "Get ready to dial 911."

Isn't it amazing how hard our children sometimes work to impress us? "Watch me, Mom! I can do a flip off the top bunk!" "Watch, Dad! I can ride my bike off the porch with no hands!" There was a period in our lives when my husband and I had the neighborhood ER keep a form ready for us at all times. I simply filled in relevant information (which kid, which body part) upon arrival. I often worried that I would get home from a hospital run and find a social worker at my front doorstep.

"Can you tell me, Mrs. Rhea, how your daughter managed to injure herself on a *stationary* bike?" "And, tell me, Mrs. Rhea, exactly who stuck the jelly bean up the nose of your three-year-old?"

Eyes-wide-open Parenting

I was at a church fellowship recently when, over the tumult, I heard one of the kids yell, "Watch me!" The head of every parent jerked in that direction, and the entire room gasped as if on cue. The only thing that would have made it funnier would have been a synchronized cell phone grope. Maybe we could have harmonized our 911 dial-ups.

We're instructed to be watchful in Colossians 4:2: "Devote yourselves to prayer, being watchful and thankful." Watchfulness, thankfulness, and prayer—all packaged together. Who would've thought those three things would fit together in such a nice set? Yet there they are! And as we devote ourselves to prayer, we find ourselves being more watchful—becoming more aware of what the Lord is doing. Every time we recognize the good things he's doing, we find more reasons for thanks.

The Message puts Colossians 4:2 this way: "Pray diligently. Stay alert, with your eyes wide open in gratitude." It's not one of those "eyes wide open to see how many stitches might be required" watches, but rather staying connected to the Father in prayer and being alert to everything he's doing, ever ready to offer him thanks for whatever that might be.

First Thessalonians 5:17–18 (MSG) says, "Be cheerful no matter what; pray all the time; thank God no matter what happens. This is the way God wants you who belong to Christ Jesus to live."

God Watching

We're given more "watching" instructions in Ephesians 5:1–4 (MSG). "Watch what God does, and then you do it, like children who learn proper behavior from their parents. Mostly what God does is love you. Keep company with him and learn a life of love. Observe how Christ loved us. His love was not cautious but extravagant. He didn't love in order to get something from us but to give everything of himself to us. Love like that." It's like our Father shouting to us, "Watch me!" We're instructed to watch and to imitate him and to let that lead us to live a life of love.

By the way, there's no need to work to impress our

heavenly Father by flying off bunk beds or cycling off porches. Staying on track means being focused on the direction he lays out before us and understanding that we can travel that road of purpose without worrying that we need to earn his love. We can simply be thankful for his ever-present, boundless love and his astounding grace! Colossians 3:15 says, "Let the peace of Christ rule in your hearts. ... And be thankful."

On a little side note, we can also be thankful as parents for every day that's "ER free."

Parenting 911

Sadly, there really are emergency situations in scores of homes across our country. These are emergencies that have nothing to do with bunk beds or bikes. They stem from parents who are setting poor examples for their children—or no examples at all. The result is children who learn from other children, from TV, from every messed-up source out there. It's catastrophic for this generation and directionless generations to come.

Parents need to be able to shout a big "watch me!" right back at their children.

When asked how parents can succeed in raising children to love Jesus, author and family advocate Dr. James Dobson suggests a "watch me" kind of parenting:

> The best approach is found in the instruction given to the children of Israel by Moses more than four thousand years ago. He wrote, "Impress them on your children. Talk about them when you sit at home and when you walk along the road, when you lie down and when you get up. Tie them as symbols on your hands and bind them on your foreheads. Write them

on the doorframes of your houses and on your gates" (Deut. 6:7–9).

This commandment provides the key to effective spiritual training at home. It isn't enough to pray with your children each night, although family devotions are important. We must live the principles of faith throughout the day. References to the Lord and our beliefs should permeate our conversation and our interactions with our kids. Our love for Jesus should be understood to be the first priority in our lives. We must miss no opportunities to teach the components of our theology and the passion that is behind it.[1]

Let's make finding those opportunities a high-priority goal. Time in the car, trips to the grocery store, vacation, school shopping—even time in the ER waiting room— can become time well spent when we're using every opportunity to deposit wisdom and a passionate love for Jesus in our kids.

Write these commandments that I've given you today on your hearts. Get them inside of you and then get them inside your children. Talk about them wherever you are, sitting at home or walking in the street; talk about them from the time you get up in the morning to when you fall into bed at night. Tie them on your hands and foreheads as a reminder; inscribe them on the doorposts of your homes and on your city gates.

Deuteronomy 6:7–9, THE MESSAGE

chapter two

· · · · ·

Who's Your Provider?

We took all five of our children out for dinner at a nice restaurant the other night. With the kids now ages ten to seventeen, only one could order from the kids' menu. That meant that when our waitress finished her tabulating, she didn't bring us a bill. She brought us a *mortgage*. What a relief that interest rates are still relatively low at the moment. Those thirty-year dinner tabs can be murder.

The waitress seemed pretty excited. I think she's buying a sports car with the tip money. So much for the kids' college. At least we had a really nice dinner. That's good, because it looks like from here on out the kids are going to need to take turns eating.

Check, Please

It was such a wonderful feeling to have the waitress deliver the megabill to Richie and not me. I'm so thankful for the way he provides for our family. And boy, am I spoiled. My checkbook hasn't had a balance in it since the day we got married. Any worries that happen when I'm writing a check don't happen in me—they rise up in the one receiving my check. Funny how nervous people get when they're watching you write out a check to them and just as you flip your register, they notice there's absolutely nothing there. People are just funny about a balance-less checkbook.

Any money ulcers our family earns go straight to Richie, bless his heart—and stomach. When I need to write a big check, I ask Richie first. He answers in much the same way the Lord answers when I pray: "Yes," "No," or "Wait."

The Lord Will Provide

Speaking of God's answers, Richie is a wonderful reminder to me of my heavenly Father's provision. Just as Richie provides for his children, our heavenly Father provides for his. He is Jehovah-jireh: "the Lord who will provide."

Acts 14:17 says, "Yet he has not left himself without testimony: He has shown kindness by giving you rain from heaven and crops in their seasons; he provides you with plenty of food and fills your hearts with joy." In every raindrop, every speck of grain, and in every moment of joy, he shows himself faithful to provide.

Soul Provider

Our heavenly Father provides even more than the rain, food, and happiness mentioned in Acts 14—more than just the "thirty-year" kind of needs. He is our "soul provider," providing for every spiritual, eternal need. As a matter of fact, he provided for our greatest need, not even sparing his own Son to do it. Romans 5:17 says, "For if, by the trespass of the one man [Adam], death reigned through that one man, how much more will those who receive God's abundant provision of grace and of the gift of righteousness reign in life through the one man, Jesus Christ." It's by his grace that he has abundantly provided the gift of right-eousness, the gift of Jesus. He paid our tab, as it were, when it was utterly impossible for us to pay. Imagine it! The same God who provided life in the first place went all out to provide salvation too—life in the second place. Praise God for his magnificent, gracious, loving, lavish provision!

Rich in Love

When we praise the God who provides, we testify to a world that hasn't yet met the Provider. The passage in Acts tells us it's a way God testifies of himself, and Psalm 145:3–8 says,

> Great is the LORD and most worthy of praise; his greatness no one can fathom. One genera-tion will commend your works to another; they will tell of your mighty acts. They will speak of the glorious splendor of your majesty, and I will meditate on your wonderful works. They will tell of the power of your awesome works, and I will proclaim your great deeds. They will cele-brate your abundant goodness and joyfully sing of your righteousness. The LORD is gracious and compassionate, slow to anger and rich in love.

I'm so thankful the Lord is rich in love. There's no tab he can't pay, no check too hefty. It's a rich, gra-cious, compassionate love that purchased our eternal life. "He has caused his wonders to be remembered; the LORD is gracious and compassionate. He provides food for those who fear him; he remembers his covenant forever" (Ps. 111:4–5).

On a related note, I had to smile the other day when I took one of the kids to the doctor's office. Know what the receptionist asked? You guessed it—she asked for the name of my provider! Did she leave herself wide open for that one, or what!

Hallelujah!
I give thanks to GOD with everything I've got—
Wherever good people gather, and in the congregation.
GOD's works are so great, worth
A lifetime of study—endless enjoyment!
Splendor and beauty mark his craft;
His generosity never gives out.
His miracles are his memorial—
This GOD of Grace, this GOD of Love.
He gave food to those who fear him,
He remembered to keep his ancient promise.
He proved to his people that he could do what he said:
Hand them the nations on a platter—a gift!
He manufactures truth and justice;
All his products are guaranteed to last—
Never out-of-date, never obsolete, rust-proof.
All that he makes and does is honest and true:
He paid the ransom for his people,
He ordered his Covenant kept forever.
He's so personal and holy, worthy of our respect.
The good life begins in the fear of GOD—
Do that and you'll know the blessing of GOD.
His Hallelujah lasts forever!

Psalm 111, THE MESSAGE

chapter three

. . . . .

Space Invaders

I haven't exactly verified these statistics, but I'm pretty sure that ninety-nine point nine percent of people today either are parents, have parents, or have had parents at some time in their lives. Except for maybe a few test-tube people, parenting touches everyone at one stage or another. And I would also venture to say that everyone involved in any aspect of parenting—past, present, or future—would readily say that parenting presents challenges that boldly go where few challenges have gone before.

The round-the-clock mayhem of family life could drive even the most together parent to look at Psalm 55:6 in a whole new light: "Oh, that I had the wings of a dove! I would fly away and be at rest." I think that's Old Testament for "Calgon, take me away!" Children are a wonderful gift, but can anyone else admit to dreaming of flying away every now and then?

I remember one of those mega-laundry, quadruple-spill kind of days, I slipped into the only room where I could find a solitary second or two—the bathroom. It was my way to sort of "beam up" for a minute. As I was taking a few deep breaths, I glanced toward the bathroom door, where I saw eight, pudgy little toddler fingers wiggling in unison. I think it was my preschooler's way of letting me know that while I had my own space for a few seconds, he still had at least a little piece of that space. I had to laugh.

I've known so many parents who always appear to be totally together. That's okay. I like them anyway. I've wondered if they're a bit like the objects I see in my car mirrors: "Parents in spotlight appear larger than life." Still, I'd like to see what they'd do if they found a red Popsicle on the ivory carpet, wouldn't you?

Every parent becomes overwhelmed at one time or another. It seems sometimes that whatever we have to give, our kids require all of that and just a pinch more. What can you do to maintain your sense of self when your little Cling-ons are clinging on? And what's to be done with all the guilt that comes from merely wanting an inch of space all your own?

Do a Self-check

If you're feeling selfish for wanting time alone, start with a self-check. Ask:

- ✔ Do I "go on strike" if I don't get the time alone I think I deserve?
- ✔ Am I focused on the needs and wants of my family or on my own?
- ✔ Am I willing to sacrifice, or am I more concerned with others sacrificing for me?
- ✔ Do I desire time to myself so that I can better serve my family, or do I desire time to myself so that I won't have to serve my family?

If you fared pretty well on the self-check but still struggle with guilt, keep in mind that you're the only one judging you. Do you know what our perfectly holy and just God did after he created the earth and all its occupants? He rested! Surely not because he was tired—after all, he's omnipotent, all-powerful! But he gave us an example when he rested from his labors on the seventh day. And then he commanded us to do the same when he gave the Law. (See Exod. 20:9–10.)

Do a Jesus Check

Jesus spent time alone. Matthew 14:23 tells us, "After he had dismissed [the crowd], he went up on a mountainside by himself to pray. When evening came, he was there alone."

The Lord set another example when he told his disciples to get away for a rest: "Then, because so many people were coming and going that they didn't even have a chance to eat, he said to them, 'Come with me by yourselves to a quiet place and get some rest'" (Mark 6:31). The disciples were exhausted from all that serving and ministering. Boy, does that sound familiar! Jesus knew they needed a getaway, and he offered it to them guilt free.

God designed our bodies to require rest. When you give your body the rest it needs, you better equip yourself to love your family, fish the Deep Sea Barney out of the toilet, scrape peanut butter off the microwave walls, re-roll the toilet paper—yet again—and face whatever other calamities come along.

As you're following Christ's example, remember to see your children as he sees them. His Word tells us they are a "reward" in Psalm 127:3. Jesus said, "Let the little children come to me." And then his personal space was completely swallowed up. And he loved it. When we get caught up in the urgent need of the hour, it's easy to lose sight of how very precious our children are. Gaining that Jesus perspective will make a difference of intergalactic proportions.

Do a Time Check

When you've passed the self-check, and guilt feelings continue to crop up, determine to save the guilt for a real sin in your life. Then when you find time to beam up for a bit, *energize*! When the space/time continuum is not in your favor and you can't possibly get away, there just might be a way to simulate that alone time. Times of solitude rarely just magically appear when you have children. You might have to work to manufacture time for yourself, but don't let false guilt keep you from doing it. You may have to sacrifice some things in order to rest—a clean house, for instance. It's much more pleasant to live with a few dust bunnies than to live with a monster-alien disposition. There may be a clean-house season in your future (though I can't personally testify to that one), but if you need to put it off awhile, don't let it rob you of your joy.

When you're in space-creating mode, you might find that fifteen minutes on the front porch swing might offer just the right perspective-gaining time on an impossible day. Or maybe a neighbor could keep an eye on the kids for a few minutes while you take a walk.

Do a Reality Check

Surprises happen. After Jesus suggested a getaway for his disciples, they unexpectedly ended up serving a dinner for five thousand instead. I don't know about you, but I can get myself worked up into a pretty good lather over just one unexpected dinner guest! When a getaway doesn't work out or there is some other train wreck in your schedule, try not to get too rattled. We take one giant step toward maturity when we learn to accept surprises with grace.

Surrender every situation to the Lord; give the Holy

Spirit control, and watch as he supplies your every need. Even though the disciples had to serve dinner to five-thousand-plus guests, they never had to cook up a single crumb. That's my kind of cooking! As a matter of fact, they probably worked harder gathering up the leftovers than they did getting the meal ready. Everything we need is provided for us, including love, joy, peace, patience, kindness, goodness, faithfulness, gentleness, and self-control, according to Galatians 5:22–23. Sounds like every provision a parent might need!

Seven Keepers

Need some space-saving tips? Try these. They're real keepers!

1. *Keep smiling.* Don't miss the laugh in a mud-covered toddler. Even one of those record-breaking snot bubbles can inspire a great family laugh. Hang on to your sense of humor.
2. *Keep a bud.* Everyone needs a friend—especially one who's been there, done that, stained the T-shirt. Choose a friend who can offer you godly counsel and encourage you in loving your family.
3. *Keep your time with the Lord.* Rising early to spend time in his Word and in prayer is exactly what we need to equip us to meet the day's invasion.
4. *Keep a journal.* Sorting out your thoughts and feelings is great therapy and a great legacy for your kids—not to mention future blackmail material! I'm wondering if I can put a couple of my kids through college with the journal fund.
5. *Keep a childcare co-op.* Trading time away can help you and another overwhelmed parent at the same time.

6. *Keep a rest-time requirement.* Even if your children are past napping, you can still require a "quiet" time. Believe it or not, the kids sometimes need a little space as much as you do.
7. *Keep up the pace.* Your time at the most hectic pace will be over in a wink—probably sooner than you're really ready for it to be over. Don't forget to enjoy the adventure.

Enjoy Your Close Encounters

When you find yourself needing a little space, head for the porch swing, take that soak in the tub, or maybe even head out for that flight on dove's wings. You might have to be rather "Enterprising" to engage your flight. But from the bird's-eye view, you can gain a heavenly perspective that will help you better love your space invaders in those close encounters of the sweetest kind.

Go ahead, Scotty. Beam 'em to the mother ship. The Father ship will work, too.

Then, because so many people were coming and going that they did not even have a chance to eat, he said to them, "Come with me by yourselves to a quiet place and get some rest."

So they went away by themselves in a boat to a solitary place. But many who saw them leaving recognized them and ran on foot from all the towns and got there ahead of them. When Jesus landed and saw a large crowd, he had compassion on them, because they were like sheep without a shepherd. So he began teaching them many things.

By this time it was late in the day, so his disciples came to him. "This is a remote place," they said, "and it's already very late. Send the people away so they can go to

*the surrounding countryside and villages and buy them-
selves something to eat."*

But he answered, "You give them something to eat."

*They said to him, "That would take eight months of a
man's wages! Are we to go and spend that much on bread
and give it to them to eat?"*

"How many loaves do you have?" he asked. "Go and see."

When they found out, they said, "Five—and two fish."

*Then Jesus directed them to have all the people sit down
in groups on the green grass. So they sat down in groups of
hundreds and fifties. Taking the five loaves and the two fish
and looking up to heaven, he gave thanks and broke the
loaves. Then he gave them to his disciples to set before the
people. He also divided the two fish among them all. They all
ate and were satisfied.*

Mark 6:31–42

chapter four
What's in a Name?

When I was pregnant with my fifth baby, Andrew and Jordan were six and four years old. They decided they should be the ones to choose a name for the new baby. It didn't take them very long to agree on the perfect name: *Spiderman*. Do I always listen to my children? No. And you're welcome, Daniel (alias Spiderman).

I read about a family with the last name of Cianci (pronounced *see-ANN-see*) who named their daughter Nancy Ann. Try out that combo a few times. I questioned the wisdom of another family with the last name of Moss who decided to name their son Pete. Or how about my uncle Rick? I'll just tell you that my maiden name is Shaw and leave it at that. Then there was the Blow family. They thought it would be funny to name their son Crushing. And what were the Snoddys thinking when they named their child Limmie B.? I could go on and tell you about Getta Fax, Sandy Clause, and Nevil Orange, but it's just too sad.

They might as well have gone to a soap writer for a name! Of course, if they didn't come away with a motorcycle brand, it would still be something like Calliope, Thorne, Tanner, Creed, or Edge. I've heard they even have a Keemo. Please, that's a treatment, not a name.

Show Me Some I.D.

But who are we really? Can the person you are really be wrapped up in a first, middle, and last name? How many children and teenagers are struggling with self-esteem issues? How many people are still trying to "find themselves" on into adulthood? How many don't like who they find once they do?

If we've put our faith in Christ, we've become children of God and taken on his name. That's who we are! Does that take care of self-esteem issues, or what! First John 3:1 says, "How great is the love the Father has lavished on us, that we should be called children of God! And that is what we are!" It's his love that makes us special. Jesus explained that he would go to great lengths—that he'd be willing to leave the ninety-nine—to find the one. You're the one! Your child needs to understand that he is the one; she is the one. What special, blessed love!

Placing my identity in my name won't work. As a matter of fact, if my identity is in anything or anyone other than Jesus Christ and him crucified, then I'm setting myself up for a major identity crisis. But when I take on his name, I have something to brag about! Psalm 20:7 (NASB) says, "... we will boast in the name of the LORD, our God."

Make a Name for Yourself

It's amazing what we see people do for fame. They'll go to all kinds of extremes to elevate their own names. From Guinness records to reality shows, people can come up with some pretty creative and/or strange ways to get their names out there. But Isaiah 26:8 says, "Yes, LORD, walking in the way of your laws, we wait for you; your name and renown are the desire of our hearts." We are a credit to our family name when we've learned to focus on his law and his plan, his name and his fame—when our heart's desire is his glorious renown.

"And whatever you do, whether in word or deed, do it all in the name of the Lord Jesus" (Col. 3:17). Whatever tag you've been given, rejoice in your mission to proclaim the name of the Lord Jesus in everything. As we seek to build up his name, something quite amazing happens. Our own reputation becomes one of love, giving, and wisdom. We develop a "good name." Proverbs 22:1 tells us that "A good name is more desirable than great riches; to be esteemed is better than silver or gold." Is there any greater honor than having the name of Jesus glorified by our lives? The prayer of Paul in 2 Thessalonians 1:12 should be behind the scenes of everything we do: "We pray this so that the name of our Lord Jesus may be glorified in you, and you in him, according to the grace of our God and the Lord Jesus Christ."

Bringing glory to his name—that's the way to find real gratification in life. You can also feel pretty gratified that your name is not "Ima Hogg." It was probably a pretty tough childhood for both her and her sister "Ura."

If you have any encouragement from being united with Christ, if any comfort from his love, if any fellowship with the Spirit, if any tenderness and compassion, then make my joy complete by being like-minded, having the same love, being one in spirit and purpose. Do nothing out of selfish ambition or vain conceit, but in humility consider others better than yourselves. Each of you should look not only to your own interests, but also to the interests of others. Your attitude should be the same as that of Christ Jesus: Who, being in very nature God, did not consider equality with God something to be grasped, but made himself nothing, taking the very nature of a servant, being made in human likeness. And being found in appearance as a man, he humbled himself and became obedient to death—even death on a cross! Therefore God exalted him to the highest place and gave him the name that is above every name, that at the name of Jesus every knee should bow, in heaven and on earth and under the earth, and every tongue confess that Jesus Christ is Lord, to the glory of God the Father.

Philippians 2:1–11

chapter five

· · · · ·

Hope on a Rope

ave you ever had one of those days when it seemed
your kids woke up in the morning saying to themselves, "I wonder if all the rules still apply today.
Hmm, better test it out."

We had a rules-testing day at the mall a few years
back. I call it a rules-testing day, but I think it could be
more accurately described as "Store Wars." I'm talking
about major battles here. While one kid was whining
to go to the toy store, I wrestled to keep my toddler out
of the fountain. "I get da moneys." If I'd realized how
much lunch was going to cost, I might've let her go in
after them.

By noon I had chased kids in and out of more stores
than I could count. I'd also cleaned up a ketchup disaster that would not have been viewable for anyone
with a weak constitution (it's amazing how far those
little packets can squirt when pounced on by two four-
year-old feet). I won't even tell you about the diaper
situation. Okay, I'll tell you this much: when you hold
a baby on your hip, and that baby is wearing a diaper
way past full, don't be surprised if one of your shoes
squishes for about two hours afterward.

The Ties That Bind

The stories my dad and his siblings tell make my experience at the mall look like a stroll in the park. They were all a tad unruly. By "a tad unruly" I mean that my grandmother was probably pretty happy every day that went by with no criminal charges filed against any of her babies. When the kids had given her all she could handle and she was at the end of her rope, she would literally tie them all to her with a nice, strong, extra-thick length of twine. Needless to say, that was in the days before toddler harnesses were readily available and social workers a bit less vigilant (just kidding). It was just my grandmother's way of ensuring all the kids made it home with her. They must've looked like a family of mountain climbers.

Hope for the Rope-less

Ever feel like you're at the end of your rope? There's hope for you! As a matter of fact, coming to the end of your rope can actually be a good thing. A. W. Tozer said, "The reason why many are still troubled, still seeking, still making little forward progress is because they haven't yet come to the end of themselves. We're still trying to give orders, and interfering with God's work within us." Sometimes coming to the end of our rope means coming to the end of ourselves. It's the place where we strip away pride and get out of the way of what God would like to accomplish in us and through us.

Self-sufficiency is the enemy of the hope Christ wants to build in our lives through our reliance on him. Philippians 4:13 (AB) says, "I am ready for anything and equal to anything through Him who infuses inner strength into me, that is, I am self-sufficient in Christ's sufficiency." There's only one kind of sufficiency we need to have: His.

Come to Your Senses

Get to the end of yourself and you'll find hope there. In Jesus' parable of the prodigal son, the straying son came to a place of revelation.

"There was a man who had two sons. The younger one said to his father, 'Father, give me my share of the estate.' So he divided his property between them.

"Not long after that, the younger son got together all he had, set off for a distant country and there squandered his wealth in wild living. After he had spent everything, there was a severe famine in that whole country, and he began to be in need. So he went and hired himself out to a citizen of that country, who sent him to his fields to feed pigs. He longed to fill his stomach with the pods that the pigs were eating, but no one gave him anything.

"When he came to his senses, he said, 'How many of my father's hired men have food to spare, and here I am starving to death!' ... So he got up and went to his father.

"But while he was still a long way off, his father saw him and was filled with compassion for him; he ran to his son, threw his arms around him and kissed him." (Luke 15:11–17, 20)

The son's revelation came when he came to the end of his rope, the end of himself. It says in verse 17 that "he came to his senses." When he came to his senses, he knew where to run. He ran to his father. And one of the most beautiful pictures in God's Word is the part of the story when the father ran to his son. He embraced him, restored him, and showed him grace, mercy, and great love.

God's Love Rules

Where should we run? To our heavenly Father! In Matthew 5:3 (MSG), Jesus said, "You're blessed when you're at the end of your rope. With less of you there is more of God and his rule."

Keep holding on to the rope and what do we end up with? Rope. But let go and we learn how thrilling life is under God's rule. And we can get a new thrill every day knowing that all his rules still apply!

"You're blessed when you're at the end of your rope. With less of you there is more of God and his rule.

"You're blessed when you feel you've lost what is most dear to you. Only then can you be embraced by the One most dear to you.

"You're blessed when you're content with just who you are—no more, no less. That's the moment you find your-selves proud owners of everything that can't be bought.

"You're blessed when you've worked up a good appetite for God. He's food and drink in the best meal you'll ever eat.

"You're blessed when you care. At the moment of being 'care-full,' you find yourselves cared for.

"You're blessed when you get your inside world—your mind and heart—put right. Then you can see God in the out-side world.

"You're blessed when you can show people how to cooper-ate instead of compete or fight. That's when you discover who you really are, and your place in God's family.

"*You're blessed when your commitment to God provokes persecution. The persecution drives you even deeper into God's kingdom.*

"*Not only that—count yourselves blessed every time people put you down or throw you out or speak lies about you to discredit me. What it means is that the truth is too close for comfort and they are uncomfortable. You can be glad when that happens—give a cheer, even!—for though they don't like it, I do! And all heaven applauds. And know that you are in good company. My prophets and witnesses have always gotten into this kind of trouble.*"

Matthew 5:3–12, THE MESSAGE

part two

A Dash of This, a Dash of That

Dealing with the Busyness of Life

chapter six

Help, I Need a Clone!

I'm beside myself with curiosity over the whole clone issue. Get it? Beside myself? Okay, I'm really not for going the Frankenstein route. Matters of creation are better left to the Creator. But every now and then I have one of those mornings. I remember one of them vividly:

The alarm had been set for PM instead of AM—again. I bolted out of bed and gave my husband a whopping (yet loving) jab to the ribcage. We both darted madly around the house, rousing kids and tossing clothes at them. I made it to the kitchen in record time, just to discover we were out of milk—except for that container way in the back of the fridge. Scary. The milk was a little gristly, but what could I do? I shrugged it off as concentrated calcium and added more Fructose Krunchies.

The kids spouted needs at me as I tried to build five lunches from six slices of bread, three stale crackers, four slices of bologna, and a Ho Ho—definitely a bad grocery morning.

Then there was the list. My oldest son needed a ride to basketball practice—and yet another bottle of hair gel. Another had an orthodontist appointment. But wait, basketball practice would be over while I was still at the orthodontist's office. And the eight-year-old had a piano lesson at the exact same time. Another child had to have reeds for her clarinet by noon and some sort of permission slip I should have signed last week. Still another needed to study his spelling list before leaving for school. It was all those "ei" and "ie" words, and I realized I was going to have to study, too. We were both having a tough time concentrating. I was stretching bologna. He was excited about a party invitation. Of course, the party started at the same time as the basketball-orthodontist-piano-lesson schedule disaster. It was all making me dizzy. I thought, *I need a doctor.* Then I thought, *I need a clone! IS THERE A GENETICIST IN THE HOUSE?*

I know I'm not the only one trying to divide myself among the kids when they are making countless demands and all of them need one-on-one time at the same time. Many of us have been there, spreading ourselves a little too thin. How can we divide ourselves among our children without falling apart?

Analyze Your Activities

It never hurts to be organized. I keep meaning to try it myself. It's even happened accidentally a time or two. Squeezing the grocery store run between piano lessons and orthodontist appointments can be tricky, but we get a little more creative when we're trying to lessen our clone need, don't we? Any place we can keep ourselves from doubling back in those road trips can help. (Did I say "doubling back"?)

You can try it, too. Take a look at your list of activities. Is there any fluff that can be cut out? It's okay to say no now and then for sanity's sake. Let your daughter know that soccer won't fit into the schedule this time around, but maybe she can try again next season. You may have to leave out some of your own favorite activities, too. While a golf lesson might not fit now, remember that you can plug it back in when the mayhem lets up.

Itemize Your List

Speaking of mayhem, I can't do anything without checking my calendar. It's close to impossible to keep up with today's kind of chaos without writing everything down. Frustration builds when we're missing appointments and activities, and we tend to make a lot more of those unnecessary trips. Forgetting the dry-cleaning and the reeds can cost two more trips we just don't have time for. We can avoid some of those calendar train wrecks by keeping a to-do list and a schedule close at hand.

Keeping up with our lists can also help us carve quality time out of the schedule. Even time in the car can become an enjoyable opportunity to chat. Think of some questions you'd like to ask your kids about school, their friends, and so on. Take one child with you when you run an errand. It's great one-on-one time. Next trip, take the other child. They can't escape conversation in the car—where are they going to run?

Mobilize Your Forces

When you can't photocopy yourself, try recruiting help. Call Grandma. Grandmas are, as my kids would say, "the bomb." The Rent-a-Grandma number should be 1-800-GRAN-AID. Maybe you don't have a grandma handy who can lend you some aid. Adopt one. There are plenty of ready-made grandparents just waiting to have a nice family take advantage of them, exploit them, and manipulate them. Actually, it can be a ministry to that stand-in grandparent, believe it or not. They might love ministering to a family like yours.

Friends, neighbors, or other relatives might fit the bill. Don't be too proud to ask for help when you need it. You can also share the load with friends in similar pickles. If you're a single parent and a grandma isn't an option, try trading off with other busy parents. Trading help can be a multiple blessing.

Realize Your Limitations

What happens when you haven't quite gotten a handle on genetic duplication, but you continue doing double duty? In his book *Parenting Isn't for Cowards,* psychologist and author Dr. James Dobson says, "... when one's body is finally exhausted, an interesting thing happens to the emotions. They also malfunction. You see, the mind, body and spirit are very close neighbors and one usually catches the ills of the other." When we set impossible standards and an impossible pace for ourselves, we may be setting ourselves up for defeat and depression.

Dr. Dobson compares raising children to a long-distance race and encourages us to pace ourselves. "If you blast out of the blocks as though you were running a sprint, you will inevitably tire out." I wonder if there's at least one parent reading this chapter who is somewhere off the track, hyperventilating. "Parenting, you see," Dobson continues, "is a marathon, and we have to adopt a pace that we can maintain for two or even three decades. That is the secret of winning. A balanced life makes that possible!"[1]

When You're on the Edge of Burnout, Try a New Take

Sometimes you can find relief by getting a new take:

1. *Take a vacation.* Even one day off can renew your outlook. We've already mentioned that our bodies require rest. Stressed bodies require even more. Take it easy when you need to.

2. *Take up a sport.* I've heard that lack of exercise and poor diet can contribute to depression. Burnout and poor health together are depression double whammies. They're big time robbers. Definitely not the kind of doubling we need. Give it a try—you might just be treating yourself to a little extra energy.

3. *Take time for friends.* Socializing with other parents gives perspective. There's comfort in knowing you're not alone. It also provides brainstorming opportunities. You can pool ideas with parents who are experiencing the same dilemmas.

4. *Take a break with a good book.* Treat yourself to some time in that novel you've been wanting to read. Or find a book with just the how-to's you're looking for. Feed your brain and your spirit.

5. *Take control.* There's hardly anything worse than feeling overwhelmed and out of control. Some things are beyond your power to change. Learn to shrug more of those away. Take charge of the areas where you can make a difference— even if it's a very small difference. Find fulfillment in the contributions you make.

Exercise Your Joy

I called Clones-R-Us to start the research for this chapter, but they just gave me a lot of double-talk. There's another one! Clones—*double talk?* Even groaning at a mindless pun can be a stress-reducing endorphin-producer. Don't let your sense of humor get lost in the shuffle. I wonder if those joy muscles get flabby if we don't exercise them.

Yesterday, while the kids watched TV, I worked on some looming writing deadlines. While I worked, I thought how nice it would be to have a clone to make dinner, do the laundry, clean the house, and anything else I don't like to do. If my twin could take care of all that, I could really focus on my work.

A commercial came on for one of those facial cleansers promising clear skin. From the other room I heard Jordan say, "I don't want clear skin. If I had clear skin, everybody could see my guts!" That did it. What could I do but shove the computer aside for a little laugh fest? Ah, therapy!

Sometimes when I'm feeling overwhelmed, the best medicine isn't doubling up duties by finding a clone to make dinner. It's doubling over with laughter! The funny things our children say and do are great solace to our busy spirits. Proverbs 17:22 (NKJV) reminds us that "A merry heart does good, *like* medicine." It's easy to take life too seriously and miss out on some great laughs when you're feeling overwhelmed. But it's just not healthy for us to get so busy that we forget to take our medicine. So take two mindless puns and call me in the morning!

Memorize the Handbook

When the schedule gets crazy and something has to

go, why is it that our Bible study and prayer time seem to get the axe first? It's in those chaotic times that we need his wisdom all the more to make the millions of snap decisions we need to make and to come up with the right responses to all the surprises along the way. We can handle the decisions and the surprises with grace when we're walking in the Spirit. To walk in the Spirit, we have to stay connected. That happens through prayer and surrender (of self and even of the calendar) and through the direction we find in our instruction book, God's Word.

Psalm 119:113–114 (NKJV) suggests we don't need a clone when it comes to God's Word. "I hate the double-minded, but I love Your law. ... I hope in Your word." Hang on to the hope—his Word.

Revolutionize Your Mind-set

Trying to be the mega-cloned, super-human, perfect parent can lead to disappointment and guilt. Guilt is a joy robber that clouds judgment. It aggravates the blues that can rob you of time and productivity you can't spare. Don't expect more of yourself than is possible for a non-genetically-altered human. We have some successes. We have some failures. Come out of the lab and join the rest of us in the real world of fallible parenting where we rarely get it all done.

At my house, I feel reasonably successful when the kids dig through the basket of clean laundry for underwear instead of the basket of *dirty* laundry. You might want to set higher goals than I have—if you're so "in-cloned." Whatever our parenting goals and whatever the number of parent clones we have working on our team, we can determine to shoot for some balance and enjoy our time with our kids.

Instead of a double, maybe we should shoot for a

double blessing. In Isaiah 61:7 (NKJV) the Lord says, "Instead of your shame you *shall have* double *honor*. ... Therefore in their land they shall possess double; everlasting joy shall be theirs." Wow! Double honor and double possessions! But I love the everlasting joy best of all. And it doesn't require a clone, a twin, or even chewing gum to double your pleasure, double your fun!

> *For God, who gives seed to the farmer to plant, and later on good crops to harvest and eat, will give you more and more seed to plant and will make it grow so that you can give away more and more fruit from your harvest. Yes, God will give you much so that you can give away much, and when we take your gifts to those who need them they will break out into thanksgiving and praise to God for your help. So two good things happen as a result of your gifts—those in need are helped, and they overflow with thanks to God. Those you help will be glad not only because of your generous gifts to themselves and to others, but they will praise God for this proof that your deeds are as good as your doctrine. And they will pray for you with deep fervor and feeling because of the wonderful grace of God shown through you. Thank God for his Son—his Gift too wonderful for words.*
>
> *2 Corinthians 9:10–15, THE LIVING BIBLE*

chapter seven
· · · · ·
Just a Closer Sprint with Thee

We were running late, and I was trying to help one of the boys find a stray shoe. I knew it would be a big risk looking under his bed but I was getting desperate. So I gathered my wits, whispered a prayer, and mustered up enough courage to investigate his grotto.

It wasn't enough preparation. Then again, maybe there's no preparing for such things. I don't know, maybe I could've taken some kind of organizational course or a Bible study. At the very least a tetanus shot.

No wonder the kid was out of underwear. We could've clothed a third-world nation with what I found under there. Next to school papers from the previous year I found everything my husband threw out when he last cleaned out the garage.

A Lamp unto His Feet?

"What is that—an upside-down lamp?" I asked as I cautiously stretched an arm to the back corner.

My son looked afraid to answer. Never a good sign.

When I fished it out, I found it wasn't a lamp. It was some sort of sculpture made out of my dishes. Why were there dishes under his bed? He doesn't eat under there. Does he?

This was a clue we'd been entirely too busy. Not only had I been unaware he had a little secret feast in his room, but I didn't know when—or what—he ate. Whatever it was, it had glued the bowl to the plate. That couldn't be good.

I do have some good news, though. Even when the schedule is crazy, even when the household is a little crazy, and even when our eating habits get crazy, our hearts can still be at peace. No matter how big our need for peace might become, the peace of God is big enough to meet it.

Peace in a Flurry

Jesus came to earth to give our need for peace a permanent fix—both when the schedule is stress free and when it's totally out of control. His peace is the kind that doesn't come and go with a flurry of activity.

True, it's easy to let the family's activity level get out of hand. Anytime we find a glass glued to a bowl under one of the kids' beds, for instance, that's a clue that it's time to take a look at the schedule and see where it can be tweaked. But even when we're struggling with an "untweakable" schedule that promises to keep us in a dead sprint for a season, we can still experience a living inner stillness.

Zechariah's prophecy recorded in Luke 1:68–79 tells us about Jesus coming to meet our need for living peace.

> Praise be to the Lord, the God of Israel,
> because he has come and has redeemed his
> people. He has raised up a horn of salvation for

us in the house of his servant David (as he said through his holy prophets of long ago), salvation from our enemies and from the hand of all who hate us—to show mercy to our fathers and to remember his holy covenant, the oath he swore to our father Abraham: to rescue us from the hand of our enemies, and to enable us to serve him without fear in holiness and righteousness before him all our days.

"And you, my child, will be called a prophet of the Most High; for you will go on before the Lord to prepare the way for him, to give his people the knowledge of salvation through the forgiveness of their sins, because of the tender mercy of our God, by which the rising sun will come to us from heaven to shine on those living in darkness and in the shadow of death, to guide our feet into the path of peace.

The path of peace is a gift from God, who because of his tender mercy toward us, gave us the gift of Christ. Jesus is our peace. Ephesians 2:14 says, "For he himself is our peace."

Peace at Every Pace

So even when we can't do much about the sprint, we can rest in the peace of God we have through Jesus.

I'm hopeful we'll be doing a little less sprinting around my house for two reasons. First, we did some of that tweaking our schedule needed. Second, I never found the missing shoe. Do I need to tell you how tough it is to sprint with one shoe?

Those who love your laws have great peace of heart and mind and do not stumble. I long for your salvation, Lord, and so I

have obeyed your laws. I have looked for your command-
ments, and I love them very much; yes, I have searched for
them. You know this because everything I do is known to
you. O Lord, listen to my prayers; give me the common sense
you promised. Hear my prayers; rescue me as you said you
would. I praise you for letting me learn your laws. I will sing
about their wonder, for each of them is just. Stand ready to
help me because I have chosen to follow your will. O Lord, I
have longed for your salvation, and your law is my delight. If
you will let me live, I will praise you; let your laws assist me.

Psalm 119:165–175, THE LIVING BIBLE

chapter eight

. . . . .

Hope for the Housework Impaired

If a messy home is a happy home, mine's about to split a gut. I could hardly contain the "happiness" one morning as I cautiously maneuvered my way through the obstacle course we call the family room. I had successfully cleared six tennis shoes, a math book, two trucks, and a soccer ball. But as I strategically managed my way past the checkerboard, I stepped on an undercover action figure. It must've had some sort of automatic ninja-chop action because it left a mark. As I sat and rubbed my ninja-ed foot, I looked around at the wreckage. Why is it that while some families have a rec room, mine seems to be more of a *wrecked* room? *Are we housework impaired or something?*

Hmmm. I wonder if household impairment might be a legitimate disability. Could it be covered by my insurance? Maybe I could make a case for a government-subsidized housekeeper. Maybe if all of us who are a tad, shall we say, "domestically disabled" managed to organize ourselves into a group, we could apply for minority status. Of course, that might prove to be a problem. I have a feeling we might not really be the minority.

This Could Get Messy

I know this sounds oh so weird, but I sometimes hope they never come up with a cure for sloboholism. There are days when I actually enjoy my impairment. For one thing, expectations stay low. I can hardly even disappoint myself.

Okay, I'm joking a bit. I realize caring for our homes is important. But it's also important to find that tricky balance between a total lack of discipline and focusing on the things that really count.

Paul was all about doing the right things. He had a passionate enthusiasm in regard to doing what he perceived to be the work of God. But it took a blinding encounter with Christ on the Damascus Road to show him that he was completely off target and that his focus needed to be on Jesus. Paul said in Philippians 3:4–6, "If anyone else thinks he has reasons to put confidence in the flesh, I have more: circumcised on the eighth day, of the people of Israel, of the tribe of Benjamin, a Hebrew of Hebrews; in regard to the law, a Pharisee; as for zeal, persecuting the church; as for legalistic righteousness, faultless."

But the post-Damascus road Paul said in verses 7–10,

> But whatever was to my profit I now consider loss for the sake of Christ. What is more, I consider everything a loss compared to the surpassing greatness of knowing Christ Jesus my Lord, for whose sake I have lost all things. I consider them rubbish, that I may gain Christ and be found in him, not having a righteousness of my own that comes from the law, but

that which is through faith in Christ—the righteousness that comes from God and is by faith. I want to know Christ and the power of his resurrection and the fellowship of sharing in his sufferings, becoming like him in his death.

Focus on Christ and everything else will fall into line. You may end up with the shiniest house on the block. Or not. There may be times when you'll find you need to let the dishes sit and leave the beds unmade for awhile while you sit down and play trucks with your child. Priorities fall into place as we "know Christ and the power of his resurrection" more and more.

Don't Try This at Home

As for the house, wasn't it Erma Bombeck who suggested we should always keep several "get well" cards on the mantel so if unexpected guests drop in we can say we've been sick and haven't been able to clean all week? I also read one tip that suggested if dusting was out of control, all we really need to do is buy a nice urn and put it on the coffee table. Then we could just tell guests, "This is where Grandma wanted us to scatter her ashes."

Now I'm not suggesting for a second that you do such things. I'm not suggesting you follow my housework-impaired example, either. If I made a suggestion, it would be to listen to the Holy Spirit's suggestions as you obey the commands spelled out in Scripture. Other than that, my way is definitely not the best example. As a matter of fact, I'm a little worried about my kids following in my footsteps (which probably means ninja pain in their futures). When I asked Andrew to clean his room the other day, he told me that we should hold off on that. He said the carpet would last longer in his room if we left its protective layer of clothing over it. That's my boy.

The real believers are the ones the Spirit of God leads to work away at this ministry, filling the air with Christ's praise as we do it. We couldn't carry this off by our own efforts, and we know it—even though we can list what many might think are impressive credentials. You know my pedigree: a legitimate birth, circumcised on the eighth day; an Israelite from the elite tribe of Benjamin; a strict and devout adherent to God's law; a fiery defender of the purity of my religion, even to the point of persecuting Christians; a meticulous observer of everything set down in God's law Book.

The very credentials these people are waving around as something special, I'm tearing up and throwing out with the trash—along with everything else I used to take credit for. And why? Because of Christ. Yes, all the things I once thought were so important are gone from my life. Compared to the high privilege of knowing Christ Jesus as my Master, firsthand, everything I once thought I had going for me is insignificant—dog dung. I've dumped it all in the trash so that I could embrace Christ and be embraced by him. I didn't want some petty, inferior brand of righteousness that comes from keeping a list of rules when I could get the robust kind that comes from trusting Christ—God's righteousness.

Philippians 3: 3–9, THE MESSAGE

chapter nine

. . . . .

The Juggling Act

L adies and gentlemen! May I direct your attention to the center ring!"
You've heard of the "circle" of life? Well, my family lives more like the "circus" of life. My day planner is like a three-ring circus in a three-ring binder. And I'm not the only one struggling with the juggling act. I've heard your moans. We all tend to get caught up in trying to juggle the stresses of family plans, work obligations, community affairs, church activities, school functions, and all the extracurricular chaos we cram into our packed calendars. Talk about dangerous—it's family life without a net! How do we keep it all together when life is up in the air? Maybe one or two of these JUGGLE tips will help:

J ust say no. I probably can't stress enough the need to learn to say no when you're making up the family schedule. Don't be afraid to tell your daughter that ballet class doesn't fit into this quarter's schedule. It's okay—especially if you're still bigger than she is. Sometimes we say yes to things that, in the long run, aren't really good for the kids—or good for the family. It's also okay for you to say no to yourself when you need to. You may need to leave out your judo class this season for the sake of the family schedule (and family sanity). Don't worry—you can plug your favorite activities back in when the schedule permits. Take a look at the list you already have on the schedule. Is there anything you need to chop (not necessarily a judo reference)?

Use your attitude for good and not evil. There's power in your attitude. Accept the uncompromising activities without an eye-roll. Your attitude is contagious. If your disposition stinks, your family will pick up on that—and they'll usually join right in. Second Peter 1:5–8 tells us how to build a good attitude: "For this very reason, make every effort to add to your faith goodness; and to goodness, knowledge; and to knowledge, self-control; and to self-control, perseverance; and to perseverance, godliness; and to godliness, brotherly kindness; and to brotherly kindness, love. For if you possess these qualities in increasing measure, they will keep you from being ineffective and unproductive in your knowledge of our Lord Jesus Christ." Ineffective and unproductive? That's the last thing we need! Being ineffective and unproductive in the things of the Lord would be the ultimate in attitude disappointments. Watch for eternal efficiency and productivity. Watch out for burnout while you're at it. Be ready to run to God's Word, fall on your knees, and turn to a friend whom you know will give you a godly supercharge. Center on Christ even when you're in the center ring.

Go fish for good times. Fish quality time out of the schedule wherever you can. It doesn't have to be a Martha Stewart–type uptown dinner to be considered quality family time. Let me just give you another reminder that you can ask your kids questions in the car on the way to soccer practice or the grocery store. You can find out about school, their friends—the kinds of things they're thinking about. If you have more than one child, take just one of them with you when you run an errand or two. Next trip, take the other child. Scheduling a family "date" or two can give you some memory-making time with your family, too.

Get down and get goofy. Don't spare the clowning around. Not necessarily the circus kind where you see how many clowns you can fit into a tiny car. I have to admit, though, I've felt like those clowns now and then as I've crammed my five kids in the minivan to deliver them hither and yon. It's important to learn to let yourself laugh—all the way from hither to yon. It's easy to take life too seriously and miss out on some great laughs when you're feeling stressed and overwhelmed. The funny things your children say and do can bring healing to your busy spirit—theirs, too. You won't want to miss those down-on-the-floor tickle times, either. Those special moments can slip right by if you're not watching for them. I forgot that my son needed a ride from school yesterday. When I picked him up (a half-hour late), I asked if I could buy his forgiveness by getting him absolutely anything he wanted from Burger King on the way home. (Don't worry, he knew I was joking. I'm sure he would've forgiven me anyway. Pretty sure.) He answered, "Great. I've always wanted to own my own BK." We bonded—and he now owns his own business.

Let bedtime be bedlam. It's okay now and then to give in and let the kids stay up a few extra minutes. Weird counsel? Maybe. But bedtime is golden. It's probably not a great idea on an every-night basis, but there are unique opportunities at bedtime. Kids will do just about anything to drag out bedtime and stay up a little later—yes, even talk with a parent about what's going on in their lives. Take advantage of their openness. Give your kids an extra half-hour or so. You'll probably still have some time to yourself. And you'll go to bed with something precious—a little part of their lives. Psalm 127:3–5 (MSG) says, "Don't you see that children are GOD's best gift? The fruit of the womb his generous legacy? Like a warrior's fistful of arrows are the children of a vigorous youth. Oh, how blessed are you parents, with your quivers full of children!"

Expect super success, but not super powers. We've already mentioned that trying to become Super Parent leads to disappointment and guilt. Guilt is one joy sucker and time robber we just don't need. Lose the cape and tights and join the rest of us in the real world of parenting where we rarely get it all done. We celebrate our successes; we deal with our failures. Remember the good news that when we make mistakes and we handle them correctly and humbly, we can teach our children even more than if we had done it the Super Parent way in the first place.

Whatever our views of successful parenting, we don't have to let the juggling act defeat us. We don't have to rely on the ringmaster; we can rely instead on the Real Master. He can make it one more part of the great circus adventure!

Unless the LORD builds the house, its builders labor in vain. Unless the LORD watches over the city, the watchmen stand guard in vain. In vain you rise early and stay up late, toiling for food to eat—for he grants sleep to those he loves. Sons are a heritage from the LORD, children a reward from him. Like arrows in the hands of a warrior are sons born in one's youth. Blessed is the man whose quiver is full of them. They will not be put to shame when they contend with their enemies in the gate.

Blessed are all who fear the LORD, who walk in his ways. You will eat the fruit of your labor; blessings and prosperity will be yours. Your wife will be like a fruitful vine within your house; your sons will be like olive shoots around your table. Thus is the man blessed who fears the LORD. May the LORD bless you from Zion all the days of your life; may you see the prosperity of Jerusalem, and may you live to see your children's children. Peace be upon Israel.

Psalm 127:1–128:6

chapter ten

· · · · ·

Running in Place vs. Stepping in Grace

I didn't take very many ballet classes when I was a girl. Don't worry—I'm not planning to start now. Especially since a tutu won't quite cut it anymore. It would take more of an "eight-eight" and mostly because of everything I "ate-ate." But I was always so impressed with those girls who stuck with it. I'm still amazed when I see a ballerina gliding gracefully across the floor, leaping, but never seeming to touch the ground.

The last time I tried that, I definitely touched the ground. Really hard. And it touched me back. Really hard. After a few broken lamps and a few near-broken bones, my mom decided I might be better off leaving the leaping to the professionals—and to various lizard-type creatures. I took up the flute instead. And I hardly ever got hurt on it.

Leaping Lizards

Now that I'm a mom with five kids, I know more about leaping than I ever thought I would. Aside from several unplanned lizard encounters (I have three boys, you know), I'm always hopping from one place to another—usually without ever leaving my minivan. It's a little weird to think about going to so many places, yet forever sitting in the very same seat. Can you run in place—in a car?

Have you ever noticed when you get too busy that it becomes awfully easy to slip into keep-it-together mode? You become a little less concerned with what you're accomplishing and all too concerned with simply getting it done.

Keeping Time

We "spend" our time. We exchange it for something. We may spend time foolishly on things that don't matter—running-in-place kinds of things—or we may spend our time on those things that really count. Most of us spend a little on both. As the Holy Spirit works in our lives, we move closer and closer toward spending more time in his will and less on fruitless activities.

Just as it's important for a dancer to keep time with the music, we need to keep time, too. When we rely on Christ to get sin out of the way, and keep our lives centered on his desires for us, our time can be exchanged for something of value—eternal value. Ephesians 5:15–17 says, "Be very careful, then, how you live—not as unwise but as wise, making the most of every opportunity, because the days are evil. Therefore do not be foolish, but understand what the Lord's will is."

Steps of Grace

Doing things our own way can fill our lives with foolish, empty busyness. Our lives are then full, but empty. A life filled with mere busyness is a fruitless life. It's like trying to win a race by running in place. You might be working really hard, but you're not getting anywhere. But understanding the Lord's will is giving our time to him, trusting him with every millisecond. That's putting on our spiritual dancing shoes and taking confident steps of grace—his grace.

We learn in 1 Peter 4:1–3 that time spent on the foolishness of sin has no place in a life of grace. We're instructed to live for and live in the will of God. "Therefore, since Christ suffered in his body, arm yourselves also with the same attitude, because he who has suffered in his body is done with sin. As a result, he does not live the rest of his earthly life for evil human desires, but rather for the will of God. For you have spent enough time in the past doing what pagans choose to do—living in debauchery, lust, drunkenness, orgies, carousing and detestable idolatry." Even in the midst of family pandemonium, we can say no to evil and let our lives demonstrate moves of grace.

I've Got Chaos—and I Know How to Use It!

The Lord can work through even the busiest times. He can use the busyness to show us what's really important—and what's not. And he gives grace to handle whatever dances into our lives. Ballerina grace—only better! It's grace without the leotard!

You groped your way through that murk once, but no longer. You're out in the open now. The bright light of Christ makes your way plain. So no more stumbling around. Get on with it! The good, the right, the true—these are the actions appropriate for daylight hours. Figure out what will please Christ, and then do it.

Don't waste your time on useless work, mere busywork, the barren pursuits of darkness. Expose these things for the sham they are. It's a scandal when people waste their lives on things they must do in the darkness where no one will see. Rip the cover off those frauds and see how attractive they look in the light of Christ.

Wake up from your sleep,
Climb out of your coffins;
Christ will show you the light!

So watch your step. Use your head. Make the most of every chance you get. These are desperate times!

Don't live carelessly, unthinkingly. Make sure you understand what the Master wants.

Ephesians 5:8–17, THE MESSAGE

part three

Blending Together Thoroughly

*Keeping Christ at the Center of
Every Relationship*

chapter eleven
. . . . .
Lord of My Rings

It was the day before my wedding. So what was I doing? I was watching as my husband-to-be stood in the church's giant garbage dumpster, digging through not-so-holy trash. Ah, love. I decided not to have the photographer immortalize the moment in a photo. Okay, he wasn't there anyway. But even if he had been there to capture the scene, it would've been too tough to decide where to place that photo in the wedding album. Let's see ... there's the shot of the flowers, the bridesmaids, the groomsmen, the bride tossing the bouquet, the groom standing in garbage. ... See? It sort of messes up the wedding photo flow. I was in too big of a panic to think of photos anyway. I was just this side of foaming at the mouth.

With This Ring

Richie said he had wrapped my wedding ring in a little piece of blue tissue paper and left in on his dresser. But he had looked high. He had looked low. He had looked over, under, around, and through. He had looked in his own garbage. He had looked everywhere. The man had looked for this wedding ring inside his shoes, for crying out loud.

He decided he must've vacuumed it up. So we went through the contents of the vacuum cleaner bag, dirt clod by dirt clod. We found forty-three cents, seven M&Ms, and enough lint to knit a very large, gray sweater, but no ring. Did I mention we were getting married the next day?

We finally figured that as he was cleaning his apartment getting ready for wedding company, he must've accidentally thrown away the little piece of tissue paper. Richie served on staff at the church where we were getting married and lived next door. He had already taken out his garbage, so we headed to the next logical place— the dumpster at church where he had taken it.

Ring Those Wedding Bells

Here's an interesting piece of information that I hope no one else can ever use: there's only so much time a couple (and a few close friends in the wedding party) can spend in a trash dumpster the day before their wedding before they give it up (the search, not the wedding).

I de-foamed and we walked back to his apartment. We decided that the marriage wouldn't be made or broken on a ring. The marriage was to be based on a covenant—a forever, unbreakable, un-misplaceable promise. And more than twenty years later, I'm happy to tell you that it took.

In Mark 10:6–9 Jesus said, "But at the beginning of creation God 'made them male and female.' 'For this reason a man will leave his father and mother and be united to his wife, and the two will become one flesh.' So they are no longer two, but one. Therefore what God has joined together, let man not separate."

The wedding was really to be a work of God. We weren't going to let any man separate it. We decided to let no garbage separate it, either. It's so easy to foam up over temporary things. But when the foam blew over, we saw clearly that it was the marriage we were looking forward to, not the ring.

On a Ring and a Prayer

Oneness happens when we understand that marriage is to be a picture of Christ's love for us. Jesus is our perfect example of how we should love each other—unselfishly serving. God's Word tells us in Philippians 2:3–8 (TLB),

> Don't be selfish; don't live to make a good impression on others. Be humble, thinking of others as better than yourself. Don't just think about your own affairs, but be interested in others, too, and in what they are doing. Your attitude should be the kind that was shown us by Jesus Christ, who, though he was God, did not demand and cling to his rights as God, but laid aside his mighty power and glory, taking the disguise of a slave and becoming like men. And he humbled himself even further, going so far as actually to die a criminal's death on a cross.

Those are words to live by. Those are words to stay married by. Those are even words to bless our children by. When Christ is at the center of our marriage and we love each other unconditionally, our kids pick up on it. We can give our children the priceless gift of security when we let the Lord work in our lives and in our marriages his way.

Happily Ever After

We stay better connected to each other as we stay connected to Jesus. Will we always agree? Never get frustrated with each other? Let's be realistic. But as we put on the love of Christ—his unselfishness, his kindness, his unconditional love—and we work to let the Lord make our marriage look more like his love for us, we really can live happily ever after—all glory to God!

By the way, you'll never guess what happened when we got back to Richie's apartment that day before our wedding. I looked on his dresser one more time and ... *there was my ring!* It was wrapped in a piece of *white* tissue, not *blue*. To think I wasted all that foam on non-existent blue tissue.

Our marriage is the strongest at those times when we're careful not to misplace the most important issue—our spiritual connection in Christ. (I said "issue," not "tissue.")

If you have any encouragement from being united with Christ, if any comfort from his love, if any fellowship with the Spirit, if any tenderness and compassion, then make my joy complete by being like-minded, having the same love, being one in spirit and purpose. Do nothing out of selfish ambition or vain conceit, but in humility consider others better than yourselves. Each of you should look not only to your own interests, but also to the interests of others. Your attitude should be the same as that of Christ Jesus: Who, being in very nature God, did not consider equality with God something to be grasped, but made himself nothing, taking the very nature of a servant, being made in human likeness. And being found in appearance as a man, he humbled himself and became obedient to death—even death on a cross! Therefore God exalted him to the highest place and gave him the name that is above every name, that at the name of Jesus every knee should bow, in heaven and on earth and under the earth, and every tongue confess that Jesus Christ is Lord, to the glory of God the Father.

Philippians 2:1–11

chapter twelve

· · · · ·

Marriage . . . and Other Great Experiments

arriage is definitely a step of faith. Don't you think it's probably the great experiment? "Will he be as sweet one month after the marriage as he was one month before?" "Will she use my razor?" "Will he roll the toothpaste from the bottom, or will he turn out to be one of those dreaded middle-squeezers?" "Can she learn to cook like my mother?" "Can he be reprogrammed in correct toilet-seat repositioning?" So many unknowns. Such a step of faith.

After more than twenty years of marriage, I'm pretty sure Richie and I are past the probationary period. Ours happens to be a marriage experiment gone very right. Twenty-plus years and we still like each other. We're going for a record.

Franken Marriages

I'm sad to say that I have seen some of those

"Frankenstein" kinds of marriage experiments. Have you ever seen one of those situations where Mr. Nitro marries Ms. Glycerin? Seems everyone near them ends up with smoking hair and no eyebrows. Take cover! Explosive marriage headed this way! We would probably be safer camping out in the lab of a vision-impaired nuclear physicist.

Genesis 2:23–24 tells us about the first mysterious marriage experiment. "The man said, 'This is now bone of my bones and flesh of my flesh; she shall be called 'woman,' 'for she was taken out of man.' For this reason a man will leave his father and mother and be united to his wife, and they will become one flesh." Now that's one "out there" kind of experiment. The example seems to suggest taking two individuals from different families, different backgrounds—even different genders—and making them one. Intriguing hypothesis. Could that really work?

The Secret Formula

There is a secret formula. (In a real Frankenstein-type presentation I wouldn't be able to resist inserting maniacal laughter here.) This formula is the one sure-fire way to have a successful outcome to your marriage experiment. It doesn't take a scientist to figure this one out, but the equation goes something like this:

All parts Jesus + Zero parts me = Successful marriage

Summed up, it means submitting all to Jesus.

Ephesians 5 teaches us that marriage is a picture of Christ's relationship with and his love for his bride, the church. He wants us to walk in him through every step of the marriage experiment—from hypothesis to conclusion.

In that same chapter in Ephesians, verse 21

instructs us to "Submit to one another out of reverence for Christ." As a husband and wife give over their rights and their own desires to Christ, and then honor him by submitting to and loving one another, a metamorphosis takes place. It's a zillion times more dramatic than bringing Frankenstein to life—the Lord brings a *marriage* to life. (It's alive!) Only instead of turning it into something ugly, Jesus makes that marriage into something very beautiful. The relationship becomes a picture of his grace, a picture of his love for the church. Now *that's* a miracle!

The Traditional Nontraditional Family

My children are among a dwindling number of kids *not* from untraditional families, so it's likely they'll be teased mercilessly. No separations or divorces, no step-siblings, no custody questions—how will they fit in? Nontraditional families have become more the "traditional" family in my kids' generation. Do you suppose Richie and I are depriving them of a "normal" childhood?

I come from divorced parents, and I must say that I can live with my kids being in the minority. Still, not only are they not like most kids, but what in the world will they cook up to share with their therapists down the road? At least the other kids can blame everything on their parents' bad marriages.

Let me be quick to mention that, compared to my husband's, my contribution to the success of my marriage is pretty tiny. What a guy! I'm married to a truly amazing man. Richie keeps his eyes on Jesus, his nose in God's Word, and his knees on the floor. Now there's a success formula! When two people both want the same thing—to live a life that glorifies the

Father—a oneness is born that breeds success. My hubby is constantly growing in Christ, constantly getting better and better, and so is our marriage.

Needless to say, though, you might want to pray for the poor guy. The man has had to endure some pretty monstrous razor challenges.

So be careful how you act; these are difficult days. Don't be fools; be wise: make the most of every opportunity you have for doing good. Don't act thoughtlessly, but try to find out and do whatever the Lord wants you to. Don't drink too much wine, for many evils lie along that path; be filled instead with the Holy Spirit and controlled by him. Talk with each other much about the Lord, quoting psalms and hymns and singing sacred songs, making music in your hearts to the Lord. Always give thanks for everything to our God and Father in the name of our Lord Jesus Christ. Honor Christ by submitting to each other. You wives must submit to your husbands' leadership in the same way you submit to the Lord. For a husband is in charge of his wife in the same way Christ is in charge of his body the Church. (He gave his very life to take care of it and be its Savior!) So you wives must willingly obey your husbands in everything, just as the Church obeys Christ. And you husbands, show the same kind of love to your wives as Christ showed to the Church when he died for her, to make her holy and clean, washed by baptism and God's Word; so that he could give her to himself as a glorious Church without a single spot or wrinkle or any other blemish, being holy and without a single fault. That is how husbands should treat their wives, loving them as parts of themselves. For since a man and his wife are now one, a man is really doing himself a favor and loving himself when he loves his wife! No one hates his own body but lovingly cares for it, just as Christ cares for his body the Church, of which we are parts. (That the husband and wife are one body is proved by the Scripture, which says, "A man must leave his father and mother when he marries so that he can be perfectly joined to his wife, and the two shall be one.") I know this is hard to understand, but it is an illustration of the way we are parts of the body of Christ. So again I say, a man must love his wife as a part of himself; and the wife must see to it that she deeply respects her husband—obeying, praising, and honoring him.

Ephesians 5:15–33, THE LIVING BIBLE

chapter thirteen

. . . . .

Every Single Time

Our cat, Sammy, had to go to the groomer a couple weeks ago. We put it off as long as we could. How a cat can get so grungy lying around like a log all day (a cat-a-log?) is beyond me. He sleeps ninety-seven percent of the time. But he was starting to look like a rag rug—with fringe.

Sammy hates to go to the groomer like preschoolers hate to get shots. I must say, the groomer doesn't particularly love to see him coming, either. He gives her fits—every single time. After wrestling with him for an hour or so, his groomer—a relatively small woman— called and said she couldn't finish until I picked up some kitty downers from the vet. I pictured Sammy holding her in a headlock. I think he could take her. She must've thought so, too.

I dropped the cat drugs by the shop and handed them to the groomer. She definitely looked like she'd lost a Sammy battle or two. There was a good chance she might be needing some grooming herself when this was all over. I wondered for a minute if I should wait around and make sure Sammy was the one who would be taking the meds.

Cat-a-strophic Episode

When I called later to see if I could pick him up, I asked how it went. She answered, "Well, we got him done." She didn't sound happy. I asked if Sammy gave her a run for her money and she said, "It took three of us to hold him down." The animal doesn't even have any front claws—and he was under the influence! It doesn't seem it should be that challenging for three people to groom one cat who's only about a fifth the size of the smallest of them. Especially when the cat is, shall we say, cat-a-tonic?

They still charged me double. It was more than I pay to get my own hair done … plus nails … and a facial. I hate it when I have to spend more grooming the animal than I do grooming me!

Going It Alone

I think what Sammy hates the most is that we leave him at the shop alone. No family support, poor guy. Going it alone can be tough.

So many families are suffering from the trauma of divorce—many through no fault of their own. Oodles of them are Christians. A family who is surviving a divorce is certainly no less a family. The Lord can hold, even *bind,* families together as they rely on him.

I mentioned that my parents are divorced, didn't I? They divorced when I was fourteen. But we've all made it! My folks would be the first to tell you that it's not the ideal way to go. God's plan is for marriage to be a lasting covenant. But I can tell you that we've persevered through hurt and challenge. I'm so blessed to be able to say that there has never been even one time in my life when I've doubted my parents' love for me. We still love each other dearly.

Hang On

If you've suffered the stress of a failed marriage and you're raising your kids alone—or raising them long-distance—I want to encourage you to hang in there. The Lord can heal your hurt. And he wants to give you a life full of meaning and fruitfulness.

I recently spoke with a woman who was afraid that because of her divorce, God no longer had a plan for her life. I hope you're not tempted to think that—even for a second. God's plans are bigger than we are. They're bigger than our own mistakes and the mistakes of others. God can use you in the lives of your children, your friends, and acquaintances. He can use you to bring glory to his name. Never underestimate his power to work in and through your life. Hang on to your hat! Hang on to Jesus! There's a lot of adventure still planned for you.

Single Challenges

Raising kids alone is a huge challenge—just getting them to all their activities, making the PTA meetings, getting the groceries, paying the bills, having the car repaired, and still getting to work looking sane is challenge enough. A single parent has the added stress of dealing with his or her own hurts and loneliness, the children's hurts, and often the challenges of custody issues, unsaved or uncooperative ex-mates, stepparents, and more. Though you may feel overwhelmed, try not to lean too heavily on your older kids. They still need to be kids. Lean on Jesus.

Having an influence on your kids when you only get to see them part-time is a huge challenge, too. But you can ask the Lord to make every second you do have with them count. You can let them see integrity and forgiveness in all aspects of your life. That's a lasting gift to your children.

Trusting Through the Challenges

There is joy, peace, and hope available to you. Trust in the Lord. Romans 15:13 says, "May the God of hope fill you with all joy and peace as you trust in him, so that you may overflow with hope by the power of the Holy Spirit." Your heavenly Father can be the refuge you run to when you're overwhelmed or heartbroken. "But the Lord lives on forever; he sits upon his throne to judge justly the nations of the world. All who are oppressed may come to him. He is a refuge for them in their times of trouble. All those who know your mercy, Lord, will count on you for help. For you have never yet forsaken those who trust in you. Oh, sing out your praises to the God who lives in Jerusalem. Tell the world about his unforgettable deeds" (Ps. 9:7–11 TLB).

Let Jesus carry you. Let your children see that Jesus is your rock through every trial. There's no sweeter legacy to pass on to spiritually well-groomed children. And remember that he'll be there for you—every single time!

God holds the high center, he sees and sets the world's mess right. He decides what is right for us earthlings, gives people their just deserts. God's a safe-house for the battered, a sanctuary during bad times. The moment you arrive, you relax; you're never sorry you knocked. Sing your songs to Zion-dwelling God, tell his stories to everyone you meet.

Be kind to me, God; I've been kicked around long enough. Once you've pulled me back from the gates of death, I'll write the book on Hallelujahs; on the corner of Main and First I'll hold a street meeting; I'll be the song leader; we'll fill the air with salvation songs.

Psalm 9:9–11, 13–14, THE MESSAGE

chapter fourteen

. . . . .

Men Are Computers, Women Are Cell Phones

I don't know how in the world we're going to sort out tonight's schedule," I gushed as my husband walked through the door. "You're late—and Andrew has a game an hour away. One of us will need to get him there by seven. Jordan has a game here. Kaley is cheering at Jordan's game, and she also has a game right before his. But it's the same time as Andrew's away game. That's also the time Allie and Daniel are supposed to have practice at ..." I hadn't even gotten to the dinner dilemma part of my list, but I knew by his wide-eyed, zombie-type stare that Richie had shut down somewhere just after "You're late."

I've seen the look before. I've even wondered if it could be a hypnotic state. Someday I'm going to try one of those posthypnotic suggestions. If you happen to catch him suddenly picking up his own socks, voluntarily handing over the remote, and bringing me home a pound of chocolates every night, you'll know it works.

How many other wives have seen their husbands processing information when suddenly the screen-saver kicks on? My husband is able to process a lot of information. I know—I can dish it out in pretty hefty chunks. There are times, however, when something seems to happen to his internal processor. Everything sort of locks up, and I feel like I need to ... I don't know ... reboot! Oh, my—I think I'm living with a computer!

Come to think of it, my computer (the one I'm married to) also has a sleep mode. It kicks in a few minutes after the screen-saver. It's most noticeable when he's in the recliner. The computer on my desk comes to life again when I give it a little nudge, and most of the time Richie does, too. But I noticed that after a long day at the office, there's often a glitch in the system. I've tried upgrading by giving tons of input, but there still seems to be some important software missing. It's pertinent data—and I don't think even Bill Gates knows the file location on this one.

The Computer's Side of the Story

Richie trudged up the driveway after a long day of sorting out every kind of problem imaginable at the office—and once again he was late getting home. That made it that much sweeter to finally get there. Ahhh, home—his refuge, his safe place. *Lord,* he thought, *just give me a few hours to relax—maybe stop thinking about everything for awhile. Couldn't I just veg for an evening? I think I'm on information overload.*

As he opened the front door, his peace bubble exploded into an outline of the evening's agenda that could make a grown man weep—or at least glaze over. Imagine having your wife poised at the door, ready for the attack. Every word about every game and every place the kids were scheduled to be felt like a mini-missile flying from a rapid-fire machine gun. And the barrage just kept coming. He felt his consciousness slipping away. Could this be something akin to shell shock?

Do any other husbands out there come home to a major surplus of information? It's like settling into a comfy seat at a movie theater only to have your cell phone blast. Do I have to admit to being my husband's "cell phone"? I can go off unexpectedly and at the most inopportune moments. I'm also usually pretty faithful to keep it up until I'm answered. Oh, my goodness—I am a cell phone! And I don't even have voice mail!

Different Wiring

I don't know about that whole Mars/Venus thing, but I think I can safely say men and women certainly operate on different hardware. We're wired differently. The computer's communication is most often a one-way communiqué. Cell phones, on the other hand, require two-party participation. They're all about communication. Communication, communication, communication!

Dr. James Dobson hits on the wiring problem in his book *Love for a Lifetime*. He says, "Research makes it clear that most little girls are blessed with greater linguistic ability than most little boys, and it remains a lifelong talent. Simply stated, she talks more than he does."[1] Dr. Dobson suggests that God may have given Mrs. Cell Phone fifty thousand words per day while Mr. Computer may average twenty-five thousand. By the time he's walking up the driveway to his relaxing safe place, he's most likely used up ninety-eight percent of his daily word store—he's practically in sleep mode already. She, on the other hand, is ready to give him most of her fifty thousand—and she's waiting for a similar number from him. But all she gets is a busy signal. Can we find common ground?

With work, it can happen! Since it would appear all our relationships are technically challenged, why not test some of the following practical strategies and communication principles.

Instruction for Cells: Techno-compromise

✔ Want your spouse to be a good talker and a good listener? Start by being a good talker and listener yourself. Get rid of all the static—any unkind speech that shouldn't be part of your conversation anyway. Colossians 4:6 says, "Let your conversation be always full of grace." Men really are a lot like computers. They have a lot of knowledge—a great deal to offer. With the right password (words of grace and kindness instead of words of accusation), you can encourage your husband to share with you more openly.

✔ Level with your husband when you feel you need his attention—but wait for the right opportunity. Bombarding him at the door is probably not the best timing. Also, don't give him the "Well if you really understood me, you would automatically know I need you to listen" speech. Computers don't process information they haven't been given. Level—but do it lovingly.

✔ Let your computer be a computer. Don't try to make him into a cell phone. That's an electronic disaster—a marriage disaster, too. Women sometimes take on the project of rebuilding their men. Instead, accept his weaknesses. Some of the characteristics you consider weaknesses are actually the same ones you considered his strengths when you met him. Enjoy him "as is."

✔ Let Jesus meet your need for fulfillment—don't pressure your husband with your every emotional need. That just doesn't compute. It's a heavier load than a man's mainframe is wired to handle. Give over all your cares to the Lord, as God's Word tells us to do. That's the only truly safe place for your emotional data anyway.

✔ Strengthen your prayer life and Bible study time.

✔ Make room in your life for friendships with other women. You can unload several thousand words on an interested friend and let her unload a significant percentage of her fifty-thousand-word store at the same time. Women have a greater need for conversation, so try helping each other out in the dialogue area. Phone a friend—it's a great marriage lifeline.

Instruction for Computers: Can You Hear Me Now? Good.

✔ Train yourself to listen. Your wife will usually perceive your inability to listen as a lack of interest in her. Do your best to share yourself and give her meaningful conversations. Convince her you want to hear from her—if not all fifty thousand words, at least as big a portion as your internal processor can handle.

✔ Understand that the cell phone qualities that can make your wife seem high maintenance are the same qualities that make your own Mrs. Cell Phone a great asset. Find ways to let her know that you really do appreciate her and that you cherish your time together. If your screensaver tends to kick on when you get home from work, schedule another time to give your wife your sole attention.

✔ Plan special time together. A date is a great way to let your wife know that you enjoy being with her. Design dates that aren't centered around movies or plays—not only because cell phones and movies aren't exactly harmonious, but because real conversation doesn't easily happen in those settings. Schedule a rendezvous or two in places where you can share some heart-to-heart chat time.

✔ Encourage her in her friendships with other women. Understand that women usually have a deeper need for the emotional support of girlfriends. She'll appreciate your support and you'll appreciate having a little of the word-load lifted.

✔ Lead out in prayer time together and in studying God's Word together. Time with the Lord together builds conversation that really counts. You'll both be more ready to compromise and meet the needs of the other as you're growing toward Christlikeness.

Check Your Server

Want to avoid stupid arguments? Check your "server." Good communication is rooted in unselfish kindness and in giving up our own rights. Second Timothy 2:23–24 says, "Don't have anything to do with foolish and stupid arguments, because you know they produce quarrels. And the Lord's servant must not quarrel; instead, he must be kind to everyone. ..."

And here's one worth downloading: "Make sure that nobody pays back wrong for wrong, but always try to be kind to each other ..." (1 Thess. 5:15). Why is it sometimes more difficult to show common courtesy to the ones we love most? If we keep our antennae up, we can find ways to express our love for one another in kindness.

Keeping our noses in God's Word will steer us away from the stupid stuff and encourage us in building God's kind of love and kindness.

Maybe we should commit these verses to RAM!

Getting Connected

Cell phones and computers do have something in common. They have a need for a connection, just as husbands and wives have a need for connection. And isn't it interesting that techno-smart people are finding more and more ways computers and cell phones can work together to make life better? Understanding—even enjoying—our differences can help make life sweeter.

Closer to the Rhea home, I'm trying to be more understanding when Richie is "cyberspaced." I'm also more open about asking for his understanding when I need his attention on the line. I try to mention it somewhere between the socks and the chocolates.

My son, pay attention to what I say; listen closely to my words. Do not let them out of your sight, keep them within your heart; for they are life to those who find them and health to a man's whole body. Above all else, guard your heart, for it is the wellspring of life. Put away perversity from your mouth; keep corrupt talk far from your lips. Let your eyes look straight ahead, fix your gaze directly before you. Make level paths for your feet and take only ways that are firm. Do not swerve to the right or the left; keep your foot from evil.

Proverbs 4:20–27

chapter fifteen

· · · · · ·

Say Cheese

A new publicity photo? Why do I need a new publicity photo? The news disturbed me. Hadn't I just had a new photo taken ... when was it ... ten years ago? Photos are such a pain! Why couldn't we just synthesize one (otherwise known as "photosynthesis")? The bigger factor to consider was I had only one chin in the ten-year-old picture. Since I hit forty I'd discovered an additional chin every year or so. Now if I raise my head to reduce the number of chins, I get a photo that's more of an "up the nose" shot. No, not an attractive look. I figured I'd just keep using the one-chin photo until Jesus comes again (and gives me my glorified, uni-chinned body). Besides, don't these people understand how difficult it is to coordinate that one quarterly good hair day with the one monthly good clothes day, let alone get both days to land on the same day as the photo shoot? Everyone knows that before a photo shoot you have to endure three weeks of salad. Only salad. And a good hair day? That's more complicated to predict than solar flares. You never know when the perfect, photo-worthy hair day is going to pop up.

Picture This

I reluctantly agreed to have the new photo made

anyway, even though I cheated for two and a half of the three salad weeks. I knew it wasn't going to be easy when the day started with a hairdo that reminded me a little of Einstein's. Oh well, at least I'll look smart, I thought.

The photographer asked chatty questions about my family as she arranged my shoulders this way, my head that way. She put my right arm in, I put my right arm out, but at least I fought off the urge to shake it all about. When I mentioned my five kids, the chipper lady tried to offer a compliment: "Wow, you look pretty good for a person who's had five kids."

What did that mean? Couldn't she just have easily said something like, "Wow, you don't look half bad for a person who's been plastered by a giant cement truck"?

I made a mental note. Next time I have to get a new photo made I'm taking a friend along for moral support. I have friends who could've taken this girl (in the most loving, Christian way, I'm sure). It's always good to have a friend in your corner.

See What Develops

If you're experiencing a bit of a lean friendship time, let me encourage you to invest some time in developing one or two. There's no doubt that family life presents challenges. Did I hear someone once say, "Family life—don't try this at home"? No, I guess that wouldn't make much sense. But I encourage you not to try it alone. Proverbs 15:17 says, "Better a meal of vegetables where there is love than a fattened calf with hatred." I think that means that a photo shoot with no friends can be compared to three weeks of salad, but having a friend along is better than an all-you-can-eat buffet with a build-your-own sundae bar. Your family members may be your best friends. What a blessing! Having a spouse to lean on is such a fabulous thing. I'm blessed to be married to my very best friend. Confiding in your kids can be rewarding, too. But if you limit friendships to the people in your family, you may miss out on some great counsel, great experiences, great sharing.

Everyone needs a good friend. Ecclesiastes 4:9–10 says, "Two are better than one, because they have a good reward for their labor. For if they fall, one will lift up his companion. But woe to him who is alone when he falls for he has no one to help him up" (NKJV).

Want More Kodak Moments with Friends?

Develop good conversation skills and you develop better friendship skills. Always seek to

- ✔ Ask good questions. Don't talk only about yourself. Show your friends you're interested in what's happening in their lives, too, in that Philippians 2:4 way: "Each of you should look not only to your own interests, but also to the interests of others."
- ✔ Listen to the answers. Fight the urge to interrupt or become distracted. Do at least as much listening as you do talking. Proverbs 10:19 reminds us that, "When words are many, sin is not absent, but he who holds his tongue is wise."
- ✔ Show loving concern. "Carry each other's burdens, and in this way you will fulfill the law of Christ" (Gal. 6:2).

Good friendships don't develop without work. Everyone who wants to have a good friend must become a good friend. We need to learn to love others with the unselfish, self-sacrificing love of Christ. Jesus said, "My command is this: Love each other as I have loved you" (John 15:12).

We become a good friend to another—inside or outside the family—when we learn to want the very best for that person, even if it means we're called to sacrifice our own needs and desires. Romans 12:10 instructs to "Honor one another above yourselves." We're instructed to love with Jesus-like grace and with his kind of humility and patience. Ephesians 4:2 says, "Be completely humble and gentle; be patient, bearing with one another in love."

Photographic Memory

"Bearing with one another in love" means being a loyal friend and learning to forgive repeatedly. Colossians 3:13 tells us to "Bear with each other and forgive whatever grievances you may have against one another. Forgive as the Lord forgave you." And Proverbs 17:17 (TLB) says, "A true friend is always loyal, and a brother is born to help in time of need."

We need to develop "photographic memories" regarding our friends' needs, yet keep the ability to snip up any offenses, forgiving without reservation—without even hanging on to the negatives. As for my publicity photo, let's just say I'm not exactly ecstatic over the negatives on that one either. And I'll probably be living with them for another ten years.

Most of all, love each other as if your life depended on it. Love makes up for practically anything. Be quick to give a meal to the hungry, a bed to the homeless—cheerfully. Be generous with the different things God gave you, passing them around so all get in on it: if words, let it be God's words; if help, let it be God's hearty help. That way, God's bright presence will be evident in everything through Jesus, and he'll get all the credit as the One mighty in everything—encores to the end of time. Oh, yes!

1 Peter 4:8–11, THE MESSAGE

part four

Sticking to the Recipe, Tasting Sweet Results

Disciplining and Instructing

chapter sixteen

· · · · ·

Not Just Another Pretty Plate

We'd had pizza three nights in a row. I managed to vary the menu by having take-out pizza one night, the pizza buffet the next night, and then concluding the pizza marathon with frozen pizza at home. I was pretty disgusted with myself by the time I got to the frozen pizza. I also wondered if my family would even notice if I accidentally baked the cardboard circle instead of the pizza.

As we dined on cheesy cardboard, I announced to the family that I felt terrible about the pizza-thon and that it was time we became more health conscious. When I told them we were going to start eating better, you can probably guess the response. They gave me a nearly harmonized, synchronous groan. I thought it was kind of pretty.

Shaking Up Our Diet

Over the next week of research into more healthful alternatives, it surprised me to find so many different ways to eat healthy. Sad to say, not all of them were good. I tried one of those protein bars first and thought I'd bitten into a dirt clod. We tried shakes, too—though I'm using the term loosely. I even tried pizza on rice cakes—which my family thought tasted suspiciously like Styrofoam.

About that time I read an article on the real secret to fine dining: put the Styrofoam pizza on a pretty plate. A little drizzle of colorful sauce here, a sprig of greenery there, and *voila!* Fine dining! With just the right tablecloth, the family is sure to think they're having something special for dinner. Never mind that my kids didn't know what to do to with the greenery. A couple of them asked if they should eat it or plant it. I guess fine dining is just lost on some people. Still, no matter what you're serving, presentation is everything!

The Care and Feeding of a Healthy Family

There's something even more important that I want to carefully present to my family. It's God's Word, and it's completely vital for a healthy spiritual diet. Pizzas may come and go, but I don't ever want to be casual about the spiritual nourishment of my family. Reading God's Word needs to have an uncompromising place in our family.

Not only do we need to read the Bible together, my children should also catch me reading God's Word for my own nourishment. They'll understand its importance to them more if they see by my example that it's important to me. The opposite is true, too. If my kids don't see me giving God's Word prime time— even on my busiest days—I might as well be telling them protein clod bars are wonderful ... but they're just not for me.

Spiritual Dessert

Staying consistent is key, but what do you do when just about every time you try to lead the family in a meaningful devotion time, you look over and see your little one upside down in the chair, making airplane noises? Chapter 20 will give some more specific how-to's, but the long and short of it is, go short. We can keep family devotions sweet for younger children by keeping them brief.

Parents questioned Dr. Dobson about family devotions with young children in his *Complete Marriage and Family Home Reference Guide*: "It is difficult for us to have meaningful devotions as a family because our young children seem so bored and uninvolved. They yawn and squirm and giggle while we are reading from the Bible. On the other hand, we feel it is important to teach them to pray and study God's Word. Can you help us deal with this dilemma?"

Dr. Dobson responded: "*Brevity* is the watchword. Children can't be expected to comprehend and appreciate lengthy adult spiritual activities. Four or five minutes devoted to one or two Bible verses, followed by a short prayer, usually represent the limits of attention during the preschool years. To force young children to comprehend eternal truths in an eternal devotional can be eternally dangerous."[1]

Sometimes we need to key in on the circumstances, too. If you've planned a special marathon family time, but your child missed his nap in the afternoon, you'll need to re-plan. Often a verse and a prayer—or even praying through a verse or two—is just what the spiritual dietician ordered. Short and sweet.

However you choose to do it, staying faithful to personal time and family time with the Lord is essential for the sweet life. It's more vital than staying faithful to any kind of protein bar diet, though I did find a way to make that happen, too. I just sandwich the thing between two Ding Dongs and wash it down with a chocolate shake (a *real* one). Now there's presentation!

Happy are all who perfectly follow the laws of God.
Happy are all who search for God and always do his will,
rejecting compromise with evil and walking only in his paths.
You have given us your laws to obey—
oh, how I want to follow them consistently.
Then I will not be disgraced, for I will have a clean record.
After you have corrected me, I will thank you by living as I should!
I will obey! Oh, don't forsake me and let me slip back into sin again.
How can a young man stay pure? By reading your Word and following its rules.
I have tried my best to find you—don't let me wander off from your instructions.
I have thought much about your words and stored them in my heart so that they would hold me back from sin.
Blessed Lord, teach me your rules.
I have recited your laws
and rejoiced in them more than in riches.
I will meditate upon them and give them my full respect.
I will delight in them and not forget them.
Bless me with life so that I can continue to obey you.
Open my eyes to see wonderful things in your Word.
I am but a pilgrim here on earth: how I need a map-and your commands are my chart and guide.
I long for your instructions more than I can tell.
                    Psalm 119:1–20, THE LIVING BIBLE

chapter seventeen
· · · · ·
Filtered

My husband thinks that a clean furnace filter is the cure for any malady. If we hear so much as a sneeze in our house, he disappears into the basement and doesn't come up until there's a new filter in place, protecting his family. He beat himself up for weeks when our kids had chicken pox. He was just sure it never would have happened if he had stayed on top of the filter situation.

I love the changing of the filter/guard ceremony. I'm telling you, Richie can deliver one compelling "State of the Filter" address. Of course, maybe that's because he gets to write a new one every thirty days or so.

The other day one of the kids came in with skinned knees. I teased Richie: "Your son is bleeding. Haven't you changed the furnace filter?"

Nose Filter

When I was a kid, the cure-all was Vapo-rub. If you couldn't slime away your ailment, it probably wasn't curable. I was greased down so many times growing up I thought my parents had me confused with their '68 Chevy. I'm almost sure they thought that with a Vapo-lube I'd be good as new. At least they never tried to change my oil. Still, there's something awfully comforting about sliding into bed (and I do mean sliding) with slime oozing out of your jammies. I don't know how I could've felt more protected from the symptoms of the ailment-du-jour.

The Bible-filtered Family

God's Word protects our families spiritually. My husband is even more conscientious about protecting our family with the filter of God's Word than he is about changing the furnace filter. Psalm 119:9–11 says, "How can a young man keep his way pure? By living according to your word. I seek you with all my heart; do not let me stray from your commands. I have hidden your word in my heart that I might not sin against you."

Heart-guard

God's Word acts as our sin filter. It helps keep our way pure. What's more, we can hide it away in our hearts and let it work to make purity a more natural way of life. Memorizing and meditating on God's Word can make living for Christ happen about as naturally as breathing. We can't see his Word working on our hearts any more than we can see menthol/eucalyptus vapors. But that doesn't mean it's not working. Scripture is good for whatever ails us.

The psalmist continues in verses 43–47 (MSG): "Your commandments are what I depend on. Oh, I'll guard with my life what you've revealed to me, guard it now, guard it ever; And I'll stride freely through wide open spaces as I look for your truth and your wisdom; Then I'll tell the world what I find, speak out boldly in public, unembarrassed. I cherish your commandments—

oh, how I love them!—relishing every fragment of your counsel."

God's Word can keep us on the right road. "God, teach me lessons for living so I can stay the course. Give me insight so I can do what you tell me—my whole life one long, obedient response. Guide me down the road of your commandments; I love traveling this freeway! Give me a bent for your words of wisdom, and not for piling up loot. Divert my eyes from toys and trinkets, invigorate me on the pilgrim way" (Ps. 119:33–37 MSG).

So if you find yourself drawn down that sin road, head straight for God's Word. Do not pass go. Do not collect, well, *anything*. You can depend on the faithfulness of his Word to help guard your heart—and your family—against sin problems you encounter. He can give you what you need to say no to that sin problem. Of course, if the problem is athlete's foot or ring-around-the-collar, better check your furnace filter.

Keep me from deceitful ways; be gracious to me through your law.

I have chosen the way of truth; I have set my heart on your laws.

I hold fast to your statutes, O LORD; do not let me be put to shame.

I run in the path of your commands, for you have set my heart free.

Teach me, O LORD, to follow your decrees; then I will keep them to the end.

Give me understanding, and I will keep your law and obey it with all my heart.

Direct me in the path of your commands, for there I find delight.

Turn my heart toward your statutes and not toward selfish gain.

Turn my eyes away from worthless things; preserve my life according to your word.

Fulfill your promise to your servant, so that you may be feared.

Take away the disgrace I dread, for your laws are good.

How I long for your precepts! Preserve my life in your righteousness.

May your unfailing love come to me, O LORD, your salvation according to your promise; then I will answer the one who taunts me, for I trust in your word.

Do not snatch the word of truth from my mouth, for I have put my hope in your laws.

I will always obey your law, forever and ever.

I will walk about in freedom, for I have sought out your precepts.

Psalm 119:29–45

chapter eighteen
· · · · ·
Contentment Under Construction

Ever seen one of those Academy Award-winning performances in a slow-moving line at the grocery store? *"Mommy, I want a Brain-blaster!"* Do I have to admit I was more than a little pleased that this time it wasn't one of my kids? Of course, that could've been because my kids were at home that particular trip.

"Mom-m-m-my!" The little boy had moved from asking to whining. "I want a *cherry* Brain-blaster!" I think he hit every note through two octaves in just those few syllables, and I wondered why anyone in the world would whine for anything called a "Brain-blaster." I spotted them—right there between Gummy Grits and Fizzie Fries.

"It's too close to dinner," the mom said. "Maybe we can get candy next time."

It sounded like a reasonable response to me. But her preschooler launched into a major Brain-blaster fit. Everyone in the thirty-foot grocery line stared at the red-faced mom, waiting for her to fix the problem. She stood her ground.

I respected her stand. But somewhere around the forty-seventh verse of "I wa-a-a-a-a-a-ant it! Can I plea-ea-ea-ease have it?" he was getting to me. I was tempted to give him the brain thingies myself.

His mom hung tough, though, so he turned up the volume for her. Why do kids assume that when we say no, it means we probably didn't really hear the question?

"I WANT ONE, MO-O-O-OM!!!" High volume. The mom picked up a copy of the *World Informer*. Of course, she was reading it upside-down, but it was just another sighting of Elvis's alien love child anyway. The point was that she was successfully ignoring him. Her preschooler met the challenge. The more she ignored, the more froth he worked up. You've never seen such a tizzy. The store was remodeling, and I found myself hoping that their jackhammer guy would crank it up at the front of the store—somewhere near the line I was in. The whole thing gave me an Excedrin headache. Talk about your brain-blasters!

Contentment-Building

I probably don't need to tell you I've been on the parent side of a couple of those candy fits. I've also been on the parent side of a few of those "fix-it" stares from annoyed shoppers. Several years ago, I had all the answers for stopping the fits and building contentment. What happened? Oh yeah, then I had the children.

How do we build content kids up to code? No easy task! But 1 Timothy 6:6 says that "godliness with contentment is great gain." It's great gain toward building happy, fruitful, successful kids. It's also great gain for parents who treasure happiness and peace in their homes—not to mention the grocery store. And who doesn't treasure peace? So here are a few ideas you can try to construct content kids.

Check the Specs

You've probably noticed in your own children (and the other candy buyers) that contentment rarely pops up automatically. Look at the specs. Kids just aren't made that way. Contentment doesn't just happen any more than a ten-story building just happens. It's intentionally built.

In those days when parenting was simple and I had all the answers (yes, before the kids), I was convinced a parent could just *insist* that children be content and that would do it. Adding kids to the equation provided a new revelation: contentment has to be learned.

I felt a little better when I noticed that even Paul had to learn it. In Philippians 4:11, he said, "For I have learned to be content whatever the circumstances." I don't know about your children, but mine are probably not more spiritual than Paul was. We've had to sign up for Contentment 101.

Constructively Construct

Signing our kids up for the contentment class doesn't mean we have to nag contentment into them. There are ways to build contentment constructively, without all the negatives. Building in a positive way begins with thanks. When you look up the meaning of the word contentment, you'll find the word thankful somewhere in the definition. Encouraging children to be thankful is a great contentment builder. Sometimes we get a little weary of prompting our children with a "What do you say?" But if we hang in there, we can cultivate good habits of thankfulness.

If your kids are weak in the thanksgiving area, you can build strength through thanks exercises. Listing the things God has given you is always a great contentment-building exercise for your whole family.

Nail Down the Rules

Laying down some guidelines may sound negative, but believe it or not, kids actually appreciate having rules most of the time. One of the contentment rules in our house is that we're not allowed to use the words "no fair." When someone in our family receives something nice, everyone is required to celebrate. Okay, they quite often roll their eyes first, but we're working on it. It helps the kids get their eyes off what they don't have and rejoice in someone else's blessing.

Satan's ploy from the beginning was to inject discontentment. In essence, he said, "Sure, you can eat from those other trees of the garden. But what about that one over there?" I think he still loves to shift our focus from what we have to what we can't have. That's why some parents may need a "no window shopping" rule. Nose prints on shop windows may breed extra dissatisfaction.

There's a crippling disease in this country. I call it the "gimmies." "Gimmie more." "Gimmie better." "Gimmie ALL!" Promoting more "givvies" is a good way to get the focus off of self and onto ministering to others. When you hear an excessive number of "I wants," let it be a signal to start a new ministry project.

As for TV, Saturday morning commercials have the focused goal of convincing your kids that they can't be fulfilled unless they have the entire Karate Kate Action Playset, an alien-head tennis racket, and a Commando Potato Dude. Commercials are designed to foster discontentment. If you're hearing another "I want" at every commercial break on a Saturday morning, it's a good time to encourage some outside play or some other constructive venture.

Lay a Firm Foundation

Webster's definition of *build* includes "To construct; to raise on a foundation." A parent's model is the foundation for building content kids. We have to make sure we're not laying a wishy-washy foundation. I can't imagine trying to raise a building on a foundation made of mush. To build content kids, we have to start with content parents.

Are you a content parent? Not sure? To effectively build contentment in our kids, we need to evaluate our own level of contentment from time to time. Take this quick contentment quiz and see how you rate:

1. Do you graciously accept what you have?

   a. I accept what I have graciously without complaining.

   b. I've been caught wanting "bigger and better" now and then.

   c. I want everything—yesterday.

2. Do you envy those who have more than you do?

   a. I'm able to rejoice with those who are blessed with more than I have.

   b. I've sighed a few times, "I wish that were me."

   c. I'm still wondering how everyone else has gotten what I clearly deserve.

3. Do you buy things you can't afford?

   a. I patiently save for things I want and live within my means.

   b. I make a few impetuous purchases when I should be content with what I have.

c. I'm a quick-draw with credit cards and am constantly packing plastic heat.

4. Do you model contentment in your job?

    a. I say positive words about my work.

    b. I tend to be a job whiner.

    c. I might as well be on a job trampoline the way I discontentedly hop around.

5. Do you model contentment regarding your appearance?

    a. I'm relatively content with the way I look.

    b. I grumble about my looks every now and then.

    c. I'm a habitual appearance bellyacher.

6. Do you show thankfulness to your children and to others?

    a. I thank my children and others consistently.

    b. I've slipped up on a thank you or two.

    c. I see myself as a dictator in my home and I don't need to say thank you.

7. Do you express thanks to God for the things he does for you?

    a. I invite my children to thank God with me for all his blessings.

    b. I rarely offer thanks to God.

    c. I never thank God for his provision. He's God—he already knows I'm thankful.

Give yourself:
5 points for each "a" answer,
3 points for each "b" answer,
1 point for each "c" answer.

Now tally your points and check your score.
If you scored 31 to 35: Congratulations! You're

modeling contentment near perfection. Keep up the great work! (Exactly why did you read this chapter?)

If you scored 26 to 30: You're a good model for your kids. You could probably have written this chapter yourself. Hang in there. But do watch for sneaky areas of discontentment that might try to sneak in.

If you scored 21 to 25: You're probably about average. Still, there's plenty of room for improvement, so keep working to become more content and to model contentment. Take notes in the candy aisle in your store.

If you scored 16 to 20: You're halfway there. You've done some things well, but don't plan on lecturing on the subject just yet. Look at your answers again and make some concrete plans for improvement.

If you scored 15 or below: You have some work to do, or there's a migraine situation around the corner with your name on it. There are definitely some discontentment issues that need your attention. Don't give up. It's worth the labor.

Just Say No

In addition to keeping a check on our own contentment level, we also have to be firm when we just say no. It's a foundational principle for contentment building. If we give in to every want—every Brain-blaster fit—we can unknowingly train our children that when they whine enough and make a big enough scene, they'll get what they want. It becomes a contentment blaster, and we've set ourselves up for a candy fit at every outing. That's when we should go ahead and buy stock in Excedrin.

When we're going through that Contentment 101 class, we find that sometimes "want" is the teacher. In Philippians 4:12, Paul said that he had "learned the secret of being content." He knew how to be full or hungry, wealthy or needy—and how to be content either way.

Denying our kids a want or two can be tough. We love to provide good things for our children. We love to see them have fun. Go ahead and give your child good things, but don't give in to every whim. When you do say no, don't yield to guilt. A good contentment construction foreman needs to balance the "need" and the "plenty." An appropriate no is like headache prevention.

Keep Your Eye on the Blueprints

After Paul hinted toward his contentment secret, he spelled it out for us plainly in Philippians 4:13: "I can do everything through him who gives me strength." As tough as it is to build content kids, through Christ and the strength he gives, we can become successful builders.

Our Master Designer is the real architect, and we can trust him for the perfect plan. That plan is in God's Word—it's like our building code. All the requirements for good building are right there for us. Hebrews 13:5 is a great one: "Be content with what you have."

Hammer It Home

When we build on a good foundation and trust in the Lord for the strength, he can nail down some great results. There may be some sweat involved on our part, but the payoff is the joy of parenting children who are able to wait more patiently, who are not constantly demanding or complaining, who will respond to our gifts with thankful spirits—happy children in a practically Excedrin-free environment!

Rejoice in the Lord always. I will say it again: Rejoice! Let your gentleness be evident to all. The Lord is near. Do not be anxious about anything, but in everything, by prayer and petition, with thanksgiving, present your requests to God. And the peace of God, which transcends all understanding, will guard your hearts and your minds in Christ Jesus. Finally, brothers, whatever is true, whatever is noble, whatever is right, whatever is pure, whatever is lovely, whatever is admirable—if anything is excellent or praiseworthy— think about such things. Whatever you have learned or received or heard from me, or seen in me—put it into practice. And the God of peace will be with you. I rejoice greatly in the Lord that at last you have renewed your concern for me. Indeed, you have been concerned, but you had no opportunity to show it. I am not saying this because I am in need, for I have learned to be content whatever the circumstances. I know what it is to be in need, and I know what it is to have plenty. I have learned the secret of being content in any and every situation, whether well fed or hungry, whether living in plenty or in want. I can do everything through him who gives me strength.

Philippians 4:4–13

chapter nineteen

· · · · ·

Well-grounded Kids

Have you noticed that mothers seem to have an innate ability to identify house noises? We know every creak in the floor by pitch and grid. It's our kid sonar. We know the distinct sound of each door, window, and every other possible access to the house. I wonder how many teens down through the ages have had their big, bad plans foiled by a mom's echo-location?

And I guess as long as husbands and children continue to ask the question, "What's that noise?" mothers will continue to answer something like, "That's a combination of Jordan hitting the basketball against the west side of the house (around the third strip of siding from the top) and approximately thirty-seven cents tumbling in the dryer."

Name That Tone

I've been trying to teach sound labeling to my children. How are they doing? Let's just say you wouldn't be overly impressed. When they hear a sound and ask, "What's that?" I respond with, "What do *you* think it is?" (I guess I'm sort of the psychoanalyst of sound identification). Last time I got this answer: "Uh … it's somebody mixing marbles and Jello in the blender while juggling the cat?" Not even close.

"It's the Johnson boys riding their four-wheelers, Daniel playing his electronic skateboarder game, and the girls riding bikes—and I believe Allie's chain is slipping a little." Amateurs.

"Sound" Teaching

There's nothing wrong with keeping a keen ear on our kids. It's part of helping them grow up to be fruitful, joyful people. We're instructed to teach them. We're instructed to discipline them.

Watching and listening for how they're doing spiritually will help make sure they stay on the right road. We can do that by asking questions, by keeping up with where they're going and who they're with (even when they roll their eyes), by making sure they're sitting under good teaching at church—by making sure they're there—and by keeping communication lines open with the kids, their friends, and their teachers.

Sometimes we'll need to follow up with discipline. Discipline is appropriate correction for the purpose of building obedience and a full knowledge of right and wrong. Built right inside the word *discipline* is the word *disciple*. We can help our children become successful followers of Christ as we administer loving correction.

Loving is a key word. We should never punish our children just to show them they've disappointed us. Loving correction happens when our focus is not on us. If you find yourself wondering what your friends would think of you as a parent if they found out what your child did, or if you're wondering how your child could do this thing "to you," then you're not ready to hand down a just form of correction.

Making Sound Judgments

We should never punish our children just so they'll know how very angry we are either. In fact, loving correction rarely happens in the heat of anger. Abuse—both physical and emotional—doesn't happen during good, loving correction. It happens as a result of anger. We have to keep a check on anger when it comes to disciplining our children. Anger can lead us to have our own agenda in mind. We'll tend to think of ourselves instead of what God desires and what's really best for our children.

Be Angry and Do Not Sin

Ephesians 4:26–27 instructs us not to let our anger turn into sin. Will we become angry with our kids? Oh, yes! Most kids are incredibly skilled at finding our anger triggers—then they yank them for all they're worth. But we don't have to let that anger turn into selfishness and sin. "In your anger do not sin," verse 26 says. And it's followed by the instruction in the next verse: "and do not give the devil a foothold." When we keep a check on anger, we're making a decision not to give the Enemy any extra territory in how we deal with our kids.

Sometimes stepping away from the situation, thinking and praying through it, then coming back to deal with it justly can keep parents from letting anger become sin—and keep them from making huge, angry mistakes. Hurting our children in anger doesn't bring about a change of heart in a child. It can even breed more of the same kind of anger and can lead to bitterness and resentment that stifle the relationship. Ephesians 6:4 (TLB) says, "And now a word to you parents. Don't keep on scolding and nagging your children, making them angry and resentful. Rather, bring them up with the loving discipline the Lord himself approves, with suggestions and godly advice."

Nagging and haranguing isn't the way to build discipline in our kids either. It usually only builds a nagging and haranguing parent. Godly advice, and godly examples, will help build disciplined kids. Constant criticism will eat away at the heart of a child. Colossians 3:21 (MSG) says, "Parents, don't come down too hard on your children or you'll crush their spirits." That's the last thing we want to do, isn't it? Discipline without a huge dose of love really is crushing.

The Rules on Rules

Need a couple of rules for establishing rules?

✔ Don't expect your kids to know rules that you haven't spelled out. They shouldn't be expected to "just know" without being told. It's our job as parents to do the telling. That's a good way to make sure we're disciplining for disobedience, not ignorance. We're all born ignorant. Ignorance requires training; disobedience requires correction.

✔ Don't change the rules. Inconsistency frustrates children. In the long run, it will frustrate parents, too. If kids know that sometimes they'll get in trouble and sometimes they won't, most of them are going to gamble. Don't let an offense slide, then slide again, then again, then suddenly come down hard. Consistency pays off.

✔ Know when to show grace. While you should always stay consistent, there's a great teaching opportunity in letting your children know every now and then that you're choosing to show grace. It can give them a handle on the grace God has shown us through Christ. Let them know it's the exception and that all the rules still apply.

✔ Make sure your kids know there's nothing they can do that will squelch your love for them. Even when they need correcting, you can show them unconditional love. In fact, that correction can be one of the most genuine expressions of your love for your children.

Well-grounded Kids

No matter what your kids tell you, the right kind of loving discipline really isn't going to kill them. Proverbs 23:13 says, "Do not withhold discipline from a child; if you punish him with the rod, he will not die." Loving discipline can actually *save* a child's life.

Some parents try to remedy their own lack of self-control by not disciplining their children at all. But correction is simply not the kind of thing we can ignore. To ignore discipline is to ignore what your child really needs. Sparing them from the unpleasantness of discipline is not being a loving parent. In fact, Proverbs 13:24 (MSG) says, "A refusal to correct is a refusal to love; love your children by disciplining them."

I consider my kids well-grounded. That means they've spent a good many of the days of their lives grounded from electricity (TV, phone, computer, music, and so forth). Though they didn't think they would survive it (and a couple of times, they've had to resort to something as drastic as *reading a book*), they've persevered. Me, too.

Proverbs 23:13–16 (MSG) says, "Don't be afraid to correct your young ones; a spanking won't kill them. A good spanking, in fact, might save them from something worse than death. Dear child, if you become wise I'll be one happy parent. My heart will dance and sing to the tuneful truth you'll speak."

Did you notice it said "tuneful" truth? There's another sound I think I'll be able to identify!

Discipline your children while you still have the chance; indulging them destroys them.

Young people are prone to foolishness and fads; the cure comes through tough-minded discipline.

Wise discipline imparts wisdom; spoiled adolescents embarrass their parents.

Discipline your children; you'll be glad you did—they'll turn out delightful to live with.

Proverbs 19:18; 22:15; 29:15, 17, THE MESSAGE

chapter twenty
Shod Those Tiny Feet

A ndrew had his first devotion—and I eavesdropped.
I was in the hospital and had just taken a long, hot
shower. This was back in the days when we got
three whole days in the hospital after we gave birth.
These days, it's more like a drive-through. You "hee-
hee-hoo" into the speaker, drive around and deliver,
then get a "Please pay at the next window" from the
nurse as you pull out.

I got the extended holiday in the hospital. That
means I stayed in the shower as long as I wanted. I
didn't realize that while I was showering, Richie was
giving Andrew his first Bible study. I could hear him
talking. I dried, dressed, and peered around the door.
Richie leaned over our newborn with his Bible. I heard
him say, "… having shod your feet with the preparation of the gospel of peace" (NKJV). Then he smiled, gen-
tly grabbed Andrew's tiny baby feet, and said, "And
these are your feet!"

I came out of the bathroom smiling. "So Andrew's
having his first Bible study?" Richie grinned and said,
"Yeah. I started with Ephesians 6."

I had to laugh out loud since the very first verse in
Ephesians 6 is "Children, obey your parents in the

Lord, for this is right." Perfect Bible study for a new-born, I must say.

It Gets Easier? Not!

Neither one of us realized that first devotion time was one of the easiest we would have. The child was contained in a plastic hospital bassinette, after all. It got so much more challenging from there.

Have you ever tried to have a meaningful family devotion time while one of the kids is sticking an eraser up his nose? Then, from his pocket, another pulls out a caterpillar he's been saving all day. How spiritually uplifting is it for the family when a parent ends up chasing a kid around the room with a "Hand over that caterpillar!" while another one of the kids is yelling, "Hey, I think my eraser is stuck." Not exactly a warm, fuzzy moment. Okay, maybe fuzzy, but not warm. We moms think longingly back to those plastic bassinettes. Dads tend to think more along the lines of duct tape.

What's It Going to Take?

Just what does it take to have a meaningful family devotion time—short of an eraser-ectomy and a roll of duct tape? As your family grows and matures, its needs and your methods will change. While the kids are young, a sweet family time will include some of the following elements: God's Word, patience, prayer time, patience, teaching, and patience. Did I mention patience?

When my kids were little, we did a lot of singing. We memorized Scripture by setting it to music, too. The kids can still sing the songs—some of which we made up ourselves. We've had marching family times, family times with running and jumping, and yes, even some sitting. Caterpillars were usually optional, but on the other hand, there's nothing like a good "metamorphosis" study on 2 Corinthians 5:17. Or an off-the-cuff "God made all living creatures" study from Genesis. Anytime you add kids to a Bible study situation, you'll need to add flexibility.

Not an idea person? Instead of requiring your little ones to sit still for longer than they're able and frustrating the both of you, take a cue from other creative parents. There are tons of great books and every kind of devotional help you can imagine at your local Christian bookstore. Check out a few. Find which ones work best for your family.

See what kind of routine works best for your kids, too. Adjust your family time to the needs of your family. Sometimes you may need to have a lighter devotion time with the smallest children, then excuse them while you have a meatier teaching and prayer time with your older kids.

Family Devotion Days, Weeks, Years

We need to remember that, as important as our family devotion time is, the way we live our lives the rest of the day will teach our children more. It's not enough to teach it. We have to live it, 24/7/365. Just as Deuteronomy 6:6–7 (TLB) says, we're to teach our children at every opportunity: "And you must think constantly about these commandments I am giving you today. You must teach them to your children and talk about them when you are at home or out for a walk; at bedtime and the first thing in the morning."

When you do whatever it takes to build a consistent time of spiritual focus for your family, in the end you'll be overjoyed that you've invested the time, prayer, and yes, patience. The payback is eternal—little feet shod with the preparation of the gospel of peace! Andrew's are now shod in about a size eleven and a half.

Children, obey your parents in the Lord, for this is right. "Honor your father and mother"—which is the first commandment with a promise—"that it may go well with you and that you may enjoy long life on the earth." Fathers, do not exasperate your children; instead, bring them up in the training and instruction of the Lord. Slaves, obey your earthly masters with respect and fear, and with sincerity of heart, just as you would obey Christ. Obey them not only to win their favor when their eye is on you, but like slaves of Christ, doing the will of God from your heart. Serve wholeheartedly, as if you were serving the Lord, not men, because you know that the Lord will reward everyone for whatever good he does, whether he is slave or free. And masters, treat your slaves in the same way. Do not threaten them, since you know that he who is both their Master and yours is in heaven, and there is no favoritism with him. Finally, be strong in the Lord and in his mighty power. Put on the full armor of God so that you can take your stand against the devil's schemes. For our struggle is not against flesh and blood, but against the rulers, against the authorities, against the powers of this dark world and against the spiritual forces of evil in the heavenly realms. Therefore put on the full armor of God, so that when the day of evil comes, you may be able to stand your ground, and after you have done everything, to stand. Stand firm then, with the belt of truth buckled around your waist, with the breastplate of righteousness in place, and with your feet fitted with the readiness that comes from the gospel of peace.

Ephesians 6:1–15

part five

If at First You Don't Succeed, Fry, Fry Again

Persevering through the Challenging Moments

chapter twenty-one

Driving Ms. Rhonda

I thought childbirth was painful, but when my oldest son learned to drive, I decided *this* was the time for the epidural.

I found our driving times turned out best if I did my nails while he drove. My strategy was to focus on the nails, not the road. I'd pretty much decided to not say anything unless our lives were in mortal danger. After all, most of what a new driver learns he doesn't learn by his mother's nagging. He learns by driving. That meant most of my comments were unnecessary. The nails acted as my "muffler." I think they spared us more unproductive comments than I could count (on my neatly manicured fingers).

I have a friend who recently experienced the same adventure with her daughter. When I told her about my nail-focus method, she said it would never work for her. When I asked her why, she said it was because she has no nails. She chewed them all off their first driving trip. By their second road trip, she was working her way to the first knuckle. She has her method, I have mine. At least I get good nails.

You might think my son wasn't a good driver, but really he did just fine. His bad driving didn't bug me; the fact that he was driving—*period*—bugged me. The problem wasn't driving technique. It was a control thing. Give the steering wheel over to my child? Yikes!

Autopilot

As my kids grow, I find I'm out of the driver's seat in lots of new ways every day. Raising kids is a series of instances of letting go. It's a progression of giving over control. Parents who don't gradually give their kids control of their own lives find themselves caring for adult children who can't make even the smallest decisions for themselves. They're socially stunted—and sometimes worse. Sadly, there are parents who send kids off to college who aren't able to stand alone, who compromise their stand for Christ and their moral principles. Crash and burn. Granted, it could happen to any of us. But encouraging a young person to rightly handle his own "steering wheel" can certainly help get him started down the right road.

Nailing Down Control Issues

My nail-chewing girlfriend has had some scary experiences recently. She experiences a stifling fear whenever her daughter takes the car: What if something happens? What if she makes a wrong choice? What if she gets hurt?

Letting go isn't always easy. Still, we have to do it: let go, give over control, and trust God with our children. God's Word teaches us that the surrendered life is a life that pleases God. That's the blessed life—the happy life. The alternative is lack of trust, fret, worry, ulcers—no happiness, no nails.

One day while my son drove, I pulled out my Bible (What else could I do? My nails were finished.) and read Psalm 63:1: "O God, you are my God, earnestly I seek you; my soul thirsts for you, my body longs for you, in a dry and weary land where there is no water." What a wonderful reminder to seek God first, at the start of every day, before every journey. (It also made me thirsty. I had to ask my son to pull in to the nearest drive-through for a Diet Pepsi.)

There is amazing, trust-building strength in prayer and in God's Word. There's nothing like a reminder to trust in the Lord. Isaiah 12:2 says, "Surely God is my salvation; I will trust and not be afraid. The LORD, the LORD, is my strength and my song; he has become my salvation."

Peace on Life's Highway

Is God your salvation? If not, he can be. If he is your salvation, then let him be your strength and song, too. Then you can trust and not be afraid. Jesus said, "Peace I leave with you; my peace I give you. I do not give to you as the world gives. Do not let your hearts be troubled and do not be afraid" (John 14:27). No fear. It's a peace that can even permeate your every highway experience.

If I could drive (couldn't resist) my point home, we need to keep on trusting Jesus to get us through the sometimes painful experiences of letting go. I have another permit-toting son in the driver's seat now. And I have three more kids to teach to drive after this one. Are these going to be the sharpest-looking nails in the county, or what!

Celebrate God all day, every day. I mean, revel in him! Make it as clear as you can to all you meet that you're on their side, working with them and not against them. Help them see that the Master is about to arrive. He could show up any minute! Don't fret or worry. Instead of worrying, pray. Let petitions and praises shape your worries into prayers, letting God know your concerns. Before you know it, a sense of God's wholeness, everything coming together for good, will come and settle you down. It's wonderful what happens when Christ displaces worry at the center of your life.

Philippians 4:4–6, THE MESSAGE

chapter twenty-two
Band-aid Stickers and Scrapbook Moments

Six-year-old Kaley came parading into the house holding her wailing sister's hand. "Mom! You're going to love this! Allie fell off her bike and scraped up her elbows! There's blood and everything!"

How could she have included so many reasons to get upset in such a short paragraph? I pulled first-aid supplies from the cabinet while giving Kaley a look of shock and disapproval at the same time. Multitasking. Moms are famous for it.

Kaley had a revelation as she stood watching me clean her sister's wound. "Mom! We have those band-aid stickers, remember? This is going to make a great scrapbook page!" *Oh ... my ... goodness. I've created a six-year-old scrapbooking monster.*

I shook my head and turned my attention back to the elbows at hand, so to speak. "Blow on it!" Allie whined. Do you know how tough it is to blow on both elbows at the same time? Especially when the elbows are extremely squirmy and you're trying to clean the boo-boos and get a couple of band-aids ready in the same fell swoop. That's a challenge even for the most proven multitasker. And it didn't help, either, that I was hurting for her. Honestly, I would've taken her skinned elbows myself in a second—photo op or no photo op.

I hate to admit, I did give the situation a bit of a different eyeball as I finished doctoring Allie's boo-boos and gave her a hug or two. I started to dry her tears, but I thought, *Hmm, those little tears would sure look cute in a boo-boo picture. I have background paper that would match her outfit perfectly.*

Not necessarily one of my better mothering moments. But despite various scrapbook opportunities, it's amazing how we hurt for our children, isn't it?

Trusting through the Heartbreaks

I do know that there's probably not a mom reading this book who wouldn't take skinned elbows for her children. I know, too, that there is pain on an exponentially larger scale. Physical difficulties, emotional challenges, disappointments from family members— bad things can happen to good families. You may be reading this even as your heart is freshly broken. Wondering what to do with the hurt? Wondering where the justice is?

Even in the heartache, you can trust in the Lord. Especially in heartache. He is trustworthy. He is just. Though the hurt in your life seems unfair, it's the influence of sin in the world that brings hurt and hate and evil. God can't be unjust. Not only is he just, to put it more accurately justice is who he is. Deuteronomy 32:1–4 says, "Listen, O heavens, and I will speak; hear,

O earth, the words of my mouth. Let my teaching fall like rain and my words descend like dew, like showers on new grass, like abundant rain on tender plants. I will proclaim the name of the LORD. Oh, praise the greatness of our God! He is the Rock, his works are perfect, and all his ways are just. A faithful God who does no wrong, upright and just is he."

Never Alone

Lean on Christ. He is forever there for you. He said in John 14:15–18 (TLB), "If you love me, obey me; and I will ask the Father and he will give you another Comforter, and he will never leave you. He is the Holy Spirit, the Spirit who leads into all truth. The world at large cannot receive him, for it isn't looking for him and doesn't recognize him. But you do, for he lives with you now and some day shall be in you. No, I will not abandon you or leave you as orphans in the storm—I will come to you."

Rely on your Comforter. Second Corinthians 1:5 says, "For just as the sufferings of Christ flow over into our lives, so also through Christ our comfort overflows."

Stay in God's Word. Lean on godly friends who give wise counsel. Let God use your hurt to strengthen you, even to strengthen your family. He can take the worst thing that could happen and turn it into something good. The Cross is the perfect example. What could be worse than the Son of God dying a cruel and humiliating death? Yet it was that very incident that became our salvation—the worst thing became the best thing. Believe it or not, the hurt you experience can become a treasured page in your family album.

Eternal Justice

Know that there will come a time when God's justice will be complete. There will come a time when there will be no more heartache like the one you may now be experiencing. Revelation 21 (MSG) says:

I saw Heaven and earth new-created. Gone the first Heaven, gone the first earth, gone the sea.

I saw Holy Jerusalem, new-created, descending resplendent out of Heaven, as ready for God as a bride for her husband.

I heard a voice thunder from the Throne: "Look! Look! God has moved into the neighborhood, making his home with men and women! They're his people, he's their God. He'll wipe every tear from their eyes. Death is gone for good—tears gone, crying gone, pain gone—all the first order of things gone." The Enthroned continued, "Look! I'm making everything new. Write it all down—each word dependable and accurate."

This, my friend, is going to make the scrapbook page of all time!

"But when the Father sends the Comforter instead of me—and by the Comforter I mean the Holy Spirit—he will teach you much, as well as remind you of everything I myself have told you. I am leaving you with a gift—peace of mind and heart! And the peace I give isn't fragile like the peace the world gives. So don't be troubled or afraid."

John 14:26–27, THE LIVING BIBLE

chapter twenty-three

· · · · ·

When the Going Gets Tough, the Tough Get Pinging

I have a great dentist, but I have to confess, I wouldn't mind it if I could get away with going twice a decade instead of twice a year (and when I confess to the folks at the dentist's office exactly how much chocolate I eat, they schedule my appointments every quarter). I love chatting with my friends at the dentist's office, but do you know how tough it is to carry on a decent conversation with enough hardware in your mouth to build a toaster oven? The hygienist asks a question, and I answer using only vowels. How frustrating.

Chew on This

And when was the last time you heard someone say, "Oh, I got the best news at the dentist's office the other day"? You very seldom get a pleasant surprise there. Any surprises usually have to do with some kind of future grinding, poking, scraping, capping, or drilling.

Still, I never miss my appointments. They know where I live. Besides, with all the squirting and spritzing, the free facial is always nice. And even with my all-vowel language, I enjoy visiting with the folks there. Mostly, though, I really do love being able to leave the office flashing my newly polished pearly whites. My kids call it having a good "ping." I have dentist-chair hair for several hours after my appointment, but that's a small price to pay.

One of my radio buddies had a toothache a few months ago. Boy, you forget how miserable that can be until it hits. We had to record our radio spot a little early that day because she had a dentist appointment in the afternoon. I asked what time she was going and she answered, "Two-thirty." Really. I was trying not to laugh—after all, she was in pain. But it was awfully hard to stifle it when I asked, "You're going to the dentist's office for a toothache at *'tooth-hurty'?*" Thankfully, we were recording by phone instead of in studio. She couldn't hurt me.

You're probably thinking (hoping) I'm just about out of dental humor by now, but I've hardly made a "dent in" it. (Dentin? I couldn't help myself.)

Sentenced to the Chair

A good ping doesn't just happen for most of us without doing a little time in "the chair." I know I've done my chair fair-share (now there's some dental poetry you can sink your teeth into). Going to the dentist can be like going through a test. Would that be a "dent-test"?

Job is one man who really knew about testing. His

tests were not only mouth related, but his were giant tests that came in the form of losing his health, his family, his friends—the works. In Job 23:10–12, he said, "But he knows the way that I take; when he has tested me, I will come forth as gold. My feet have closely followed his steps; I have kept to his way without turning aside. I have not departed from the commands of his lips; I have treasured the words of his mouth more than my daily bread."

Most true tests really are no laughing matter. But just as we sometimes have to experience a bit of an ugly cleaning appointment to get our smiles to shine, we can come out of our tests smiling. Better yet, we can come out shining like gold! Job never turned aside from his God. He never stopped obeying him. He never stopped treasuring him.

Shining Instead of Whining

It's tough to go through a test without whining. Job did a little whimpering himself. Most of us do. When we get our mourning done, though, there comes a time to shine. Philippians 2:14–15 (TLB) tells us to stay away from complaining and to shine like beacons: "In everything you do, stay away from complaining and arguing so that no one can speak a word of blame against you. You are to live clean, innocent lives as children of God in a dark world full of people who are crooked and stubborn. Shine out among them like beacon lights." Rise and shine!

It's easier to smile when we realize that tests can make us stronger. They refine us and make us shinier than ever! First Peter 1:6–7 (TLB) says, "So be truly glad! There is wonderful joy ahead, even though the going is rough for awhile down here. These trials are only to test your faith, to see whether or not it is strong and pure. It is being tested as fire tests gold and purifies it—and your faith is far more precious to God than mere gold; so if your faith remains strong after being tried in the test tube of fiery trials, it will bring you much praise and glory and honor on the day of his return."

During tough times, through Jesus you can shine! Go ahead. Show the world your "ping"!

Praise be to the God and Father of our Lord Jesus Christ! In his great mercy he has given us new birth into a living hope through the resurrection of Jesus Christ from the dead, and into an inheritance that can never perish, spoil or fade— kept in heaven for you, who through faith are shielded by God's power until the coming of the salvation that is ready to be revealed in the last time. In this you greatly rejoice, though now for a little while you may have had to suffer grief in all kinds of trials. These have come so that your faith—of greater worth than gold, which perishes even though refined by fire—may be proved genuine and may result in praise, glory and honor when Jesus Christ is revealed.

1 Peter 1:3–7

chapter twenty-four
. . . . .
Hope Springs Eternal

When my first baby was just ten weeks old, we moved to a new city with all new people and a brand-new baby—with brand-new colic. "Overwhelmed" had taken on "new" meaning.

My husband is wonderfully sensitive and intuitive. He saw my stress level rising and knew I needed to get out for a bit. But he had to go to the office. "Why don't you take a trip to the mall with the baby?" he suggested.

Hmm. The colic combat might seem less overwhelming at the mall. Besides, the baby loved motion. And we all know there's hardly anything more therapeutic for a woman than scoping out a new mall. Yes! I decided to try it.

Prepare for Lift-off

I had never been on an outing with a new baby all by myself. I didn't fully realize how much paraphernalia I was dragging along until I was wrestling to unfold the stroller while trying to figure out what to do with a diaper bag that weighed as much as a Buick. I had filled the bag with more equipment than most parents need to raise a kid from infancy to fifth grade. One glance inside the megabag would've clued you in that this bag belonged to a first-time parent. I don't think that much equipment is required for a shuttle launch. I finally got things balanced enough so that the bag didn't tip the stroller over. *There, I guess that's everything. Oh, wait. The baby.*

I put the baby in the stroller, plugged in the pacifier, and shifted into hyperdrive. I made it to the inside of the mall, but whenever I tried to stop and browse through a store's goodies, the baby started to wail. I could hardly even slow down at the shop windows to glance inside. This really was hyperdrive.

I zipped past dozens of store windows until I was out of breath and plenty frustrated at not having seen much of anything. The mall had been a giant blur. I decided I would stop for some lunch—crying or no crying. But this was my first baby. We parents make loads of crying-or-no-crying resolutions with our first babies, don't we? Then we cave. I caved. I left my uneaten lunch, picked up my soft drink, and readied us both to shift back into light speed. But in my fervor (with at least a pinch of stress), I guess I must've squeezed the soda pop cup one or two degrees too snugly.

To my horror, the whole thing exploded into a giant Dr Pepper fountain—right on top of my baby's head!

Houston, We Have a Problem

He actually stopped crying for two or three seconds— two or three seconds of complete and utter shock. Droplets of Dr Pepper hung from his eyelashes and ran down his cheeks. After the initial shock wore off, he found his voice. And his squeal was in a whole new pitch. Yes, this one hit new heights—and very likely traveled to uncharted galaxies far, far away.

I peeled the sticky baby out of the stroller and

started trying to clean him off with those wimpy fast-food napkins. (Why had I suddenly forgotten that I had enough baby-cleaning equipment in the Mary Poppins bag to clean, wipe, soften, and thoroughly disinfect that baby from there to Guam?) The napkins stuck to him. I think the people around me were starting to wonder if babies could contract leprosy.

I gathered up my papier-mâché-covered baby and my two-ton diaper bag and made a beeline for the car. This was enough of a "break" for anyone. I was just about fizzled out—no soft drink pun intended.

Never Without Hope

Though we all hit those impossible, demanding, draining, soda-exploding days, as children of God we have something that keeps us going. For every Dr Pepper–exploding, stressful moment, there is an equally explosive hope available to meet the situation. Does hope come in two-liter bottles? It can if it needs to. Hope springs eternal. It even spews eternal. How wonderful that the grace of God comes packaged with the hope we need for every challenge we face.

We can be strong for any and every explosive situation when our hope is firmly placed in the Lord. Psalm 31:24 says, "Be strong and take heart, all you who hope in the LORD." There's never any need to feel hopeless. As a matter of fact, we don't even have to try to concoct it on our own. Hope is from God. And it's not a "hope so" kind of hope. The kind of hope that is completely unshakable is from God alone. The psalmist wrote in Psalm 62:5–8, "Find rest, O my soul, in God alone; my hope comes from him. He alone is my rock and my salvation; he is my fortress, I will not be shaken. My salvation and my honor depend on God; he is my mighty rock, my refuge. Trust in him at all times, O people;

pour out your hearts to him, for God is our refuge." Did anyone else notice that we're instructed to "pour out" our hearts to him? That has nothing to do with over-squeezing squishable cups.

The hope we get from God is like a shield. It doesn't necessarily shield us from challenging moments. It's not exactly a soda pop shield either. But it's a shield over our hearts and minds that keeps us looking at the important things in life—eternal things. That gives us reason to rejoice. Rejoicing must be the absolute opposite of hopelessness, don't you think? Psalm 33:20–22 says, "We wait in hope for the LORD; he is our help and our shield. In him our hearts rejoice, for we trust in his holy name. May your unfailing love rest upon us, O LORD, even as we put our hope in you."

The hope we find in our heavenly Father really does spring eternal. Praise him for his unfailing love! Hang on to him. Hang on to his love. Hang on oh-so-tightly to the hope he gives—and not so tightly to soft drink cups.

To you, O LORD, I lift up my soul; in you I trust, O my God. Do not let me be put to shame, nor let my enemies triumph over me. No one whose hope is in you will ever be put to shame, but they will be put to shame who are treacherous without excuse. Show me your ways, O LORD, teach me your paths; guide me in your truth and teach me, for you are God my Savior, and my hope is in you all day long.

Psalm 25:1–5

chapter twenty-five
· · · · ·
Learning to Let Go

Do you know how weird it is to have my oldest baby now tower a foot over my head? When I'm pretending to scold him, I shake my finger somewhere around the chin of this six-foot boy and warn, "Don't make me come up there."

It's a milestone year at the Rhea house. That six-foot baby will be graduating from high school. I'm sure your first response is one of shock and disbelief that one so young looking as I could have a child this old. No really—I need you to look shocked and disbelieving.

I'm still in a whirl. How did this happen so fast? I've heard that time is relative, but I didn't know that meant time could pass so much more quickly for certain relatives.

Precious Memories

I know it makes me sound old when I say this, but he was just born yesterday. You know you're getting older when you talk about your kids in a series of statements that begin with "I remember when ..."

I do remember when. I remember when I found out we were expecting Andrew. I cried. I remember his first word—which I had hoped would be *mommy*, but actually turned out to be *McDonalds*. I laughed till I cried. I remember his first skinned knee, his first tooth, and his first haircut. Cried, cried, cried. I remember well the day he asked Jesus to come into his life. Talk about crying. I even remember when he let me pick out his clothes. Boy, are those days gone—but at least I'm not crying over that part.

I remember the day he got his driver's license and took the car out all by himself for the first time. I might've cried, but it's tough to cry when you're holding your breath. I remember enormous pleasure and inexpressible pride the first time I heard him say he wanted to serve the Lord as a worship pastor.

As well as I remember those more recent days, I remember just as well one special day when I cradled him in my arms, all snuggled in a soft baby blanket. I remember looking into bright eyes that looked contentedly back at me. And I remember being completely amazed at such an overwhelming love. I remember thinking that holding that baby was right near the top of the list of reasons my arms were created. I asked the Lord right then and there to help me remember that special moment. I guess I had a little clue just how fleeting those baby moments might be. It's one of my sweetest rememberings.

The Mega-hanky Semester

Next year my baby will go off to college. I know, I know—I'll still have four more at home. And, happily, he's going to a college that's only an hour away from home. But we're turning a page. It's one more "letting go." I've watched that baby I've treasured grow into a beautiful boy I've treasured, and now into a godly young man I treasure. I couldn't be more proud. But this is his senior year of high school, and I can't even type the words *letting go* without tears. I've actually been a major basket case. He's my first, and I can't tell you how I'm going to miss him. In many ways, I already miss him being my "little boy."

In another sense, he'll always be my baby. His are the same bright, contented eyes that looked up at me from his snuggly baby blanket. Yep, he'll always be my baby. And in yet another sense, he's never really been mine at all. He's been sort of on loan.

I called Richie a few days ago and told him he was married to a crazy woman who's already crying about a graduation that hasn't happened yet. I sobbed at what a difficult page this is to turn. I loved his encouragement. He pointed out that we're closing one fun chapter and starting another one. That made me cry happy tears—the poor man just can't win.

No Regrets

I also love what my godly friend told me. Janet Bridgeforth has already experienced the good-byes of her two boys. She told me it's a wondrous blessing to get to this point in your children's lives and to be able to look back on the child-rearing years with no regrets. Not because we haven't done anything wrong, but because nothing has been left unresolved. Nothing left unsaid. Nothing left unconfessed. Nothing left unforgiven. We keep our finger in Proverbs around this time of life, don't we? "Point your kids in the right direction—when they're old they won't be lost" (Prov. 22:6 MSG).

I wrote a song when I was in the mega-baby years. It's not destined to become a classic or anything—except maybe at my house (if only I could sing it without bawling). But it expressed even way back then the feelings I was already anticipating:

Learning to Let Go

Tiny baby inside of me
What do you look like? I can't wait to see
And though I'm anxious to see you so much
    better
I'll miss days like today—we're so close
    together

But I'm learning to let go
It wouldn't be so hard if I didn't love you so
Learning to let go
All your life I'll be learning to let go

Learning to walk—you look so sweet
You're struggling to stand on your own two feet
I hold your fingers as you toddle down the hall
It's so hard to let go when I know you might fall

But I'm learning to let go
It wouldn't be so hard if I didn't love you so
Learning to let go
All your life I'll be learning to let go

Each mistake, I want to help mend
But some lessons require me not to bend
So I let you learn to make it right on your own
But I'm still here to love you and tell you
    you're not alone

I'm learning to let go
It wouldn't be so hard if I didn't love you so
Learning to let go
All your life I'll still be learning to let go

From the beginning I knew you weren't mine
The Lord has blessed me with you here
    for just a short time
And though I think no one can love you as I do
I know even my love can't compare to the
    Father's love for you

I'll trust you to him, all the way
Watch growth in stature and wisdom each day
Then I'll let you go—I know by then you will
    know
How to make upright decisions and the right
    way to go

But I'll still be learning to let go
It wouldn't be so hard if I didn't love you so
Learning to let go
All your life I'll still be learning to let go

Now that it's Andrew's senior year and the letting go is about to come full circle, I've discovered that those feelings I anticipated are as powerful as I imagined. I don't know when I've felt more joyful—or melancholy. Both call for tears. As tear-filled as motherhood has been, this is by far one of the soggiest seasons of my life. But with no regrets. Praise God!

Dorothy Canfield Fisher was quoted as saying, "A mother is not a person to lean on, but a person to make leaning unnecessary." I'll bet she cried when she said it.

When Joseph and Mary had done everything required by the Law of the Lord, they returned to Galilee to their own town of Nazareth. And the child grew and became strong; he was filled with wisdom, and the grace of God was upon him. Every year his parents went to Jerusalem for the Feast of the Passover. When he was twelve years old, they went up to the Feast, according to the custom. After the Feast was over, while his parents were returning home, the boy Jesus stayed behind in Jerusalem, but they were unaware of it. Thinking he was in their company, they traveled on for a day. Then they began looking for him among their relatives and friends. When they did not find him, they went back to Jerusalem to look for him. After three days they found him in the temple courts, sitting among the teachers, listening to them and asking them questions. Everyone who heard him was amazed at his understanding and his answers. When his parents saw him, they were astonished. His mother said to him, "Son, why have you treated us like this? Your father and I have been anxiously searching for you."

"Why were you searching for me?" he asked. "Didn't you know I had to be in my Father's house?" But they did not understand what he was saying to them. Then he went down to Nazareth with them and was obedient to them. But his mother treasured all these things in her heart. And Jesus grew in wisdom and stature, and in favor with God and men.

Luke 2:39–52

part six

Stirring Up a Big Batch of Belief

Building Family Faith

chapter twenty-six
No Grain, No Gain

Daniel stood at the pantry door staring into a sea of cereal boxes. "Mom, I don't know what to eat. We don't have any good cereal."

Those are the kinds of comments that automatically trigger the launch of parental discourse #943 titled, "Why, when I was a kid, we had to eat the BOX! And we were grateful!"

Smorgas-porridge

When I looked into the pantry, I found six boxes of cereal. Granted, with five kids, we usually have twice that many. It's typically a veritable smorgasbord of cereals in there. But the locusts (the other kids) had already descended and left only the healthy stuff. When Daniel said there weren't any good cereals, he really meant there weren't any that had more fructose and corn syrup than grain. No "Choco This" or "Fruity That." Instead it was "This Bran" and "That Bran." Granted, some of them were high enough in fiber to strip furniture, but there were still what I thought to be some decent grain choices.

Adolescent Food Disposal Units

I probably don't need to tell you that Daniel isn't a teen yet. At nine years old, he hasn't yet learned the fine art of indiscriminate food disposal. I do have a couple of sons of the teenage persuasion, and one of my biggest diet-monitoring challenges with them is trying to *stop* them from eating the boxes. I recently caught one of the boys eating *mayonnaise.* He was holding it about a foot over his head, squirting it out of a squeeze bottle right into his mouth. For breakfast.

Another day my oldest son stood eating leftovers from the fridge. "What is that?" I asked.

"I'm not sure, but it's fine."

"Fine" means whatever is in the container isn't swarming and doesn't answer if you ask it a question. But would you eat leftovers you couldn't even identify? Now that's faith!

With Just a Grain of Faith

When Jesus talked about faith, he said that if we have even mini-grain-sized faith, we can accomplish anything. He didn't exactly say we can *eat* anything, but he did say we can *do* anything. He said in Matthew 17:20, "I tell you the truth, if you have faith as small as a mustard seed, you can say to this mountain, 'Move from here to there' and it will move. Nothing will be impossible for you."

Amazing, isn't it? We're talking about a faith that can be as teeny as a mustard seed! (Not to be confused with the condiment.)

But how do we grasp an immeasurable faith? You can't hold faith in your hands. You can't see it. It doesn't make noise. Hebrews 11:1 tells us that faith is "being sure of what we hope for and certain of what we do not see." Faith is trust in Jesus, even though we haven't yet touched him. It's having confidence in what he teaches us even though we haven't physically heard his voice. Faith is having a sure belief in him even though we've never seen him, trusting what his Word says about him with a firm confidence.

Faith Seeds—Can We Muster Them?

Is there a faith supermarket? Can we grow it? How do we find the kind of faith that brings rest and courage at the same time?

The Bible tells us that "faith comes by hearing and hearing by the Word of God." (Rom. 10:17). The Bible reveals God's saving faith. Maintaining a steady diet of his Word will teach us about the character, history, and instruction of our heavenly Father. And the more we know about him, the more we know that he is trustworthy beyond our comprehension. God's Word is a great, faith-building way to begin every day. Talk about spiritual nourishment!

So start your morning with this important part of a complete breakfast. The Word of God is the breakfast of real champions. Not only champions, but true overcomers. First John 5:4 tells us that "This is the victory that has overcome the world, even our faith."

Faith Building

Much of faith building is simply understanding the Father. He is immense. He's the Creator, the Alpha and Omega, Beginning and End. He is all-powerful, all-loving, all-knowing—all! He is always caring, always fair, ever trustworthy, ever faithful. When we recognize that our lives are in the hands of someone so completely able, we realize we have nothing to fear. We can go boldly in any direction he leads.

Without understanding our heavenly Father, our faith is small and we live in fear. How scary is it to think that succeeding in this life depends on us instead of an all-powerful God? What a wimpy and vulnerable way to live! No peace. No confidence. No lasting joy. It's like living in a bowl of oversoaked flakes—your life can't hold up against circumstances. It's the exact opposite of the grain that "stays crunchy even in milk."

The more we know about our awesome God, the more mountainous our faith becomes. And Jesus fills the life of faith with joy and satisfaction. Try it. It's better than finding an extra prize in your cereal box!

Incidentally, I went back to the store and bought Daniel some sort of "Choco-gravel," plus the prevailing sucrose-loaded flake of the week. I bought a few boxes of the fruity kind, too—his favorite. He was so thankful I now think of them as "Fruity-Gratitudies." I'm grateful, too—grateful I don't have to eat that stuff. I'll be shooting for a well-balanced spiritual breakfast instead—something like "Mustard-seed Muesli."

The fundamental fact of existence is that this trust in God, this faith, is the firm foundation under everything that makes life worth living. It's our handle on what we can't see. The act of faith is what distinguished our ancestors, set them above the crowd. By faith, we see the world called into existence by God's word, what we see created by what we don't see. ...

By faith, Noah built a ship in the middle of dry land. He was warned about something he couldn't see, and acted on what he was told. The result? His family was saved. His act of faith drew a sharp line between the evil of the unbelieving world and the rightness of the believing world. As a result, Noah became intimate with God.

By an act of faith, Abraham said yes to God's call to travel to an unknown place that would become his home. When he left he had no idea where he was going. By an act of faith he lived in the country promised him, lived as a stranger camping in tents. Isaac and Jacob did the same, living under the same promise. Abraham did it by keeping his eye on an unseen city with real, eternal foundations—the City designed and built by God. ...

Each one of these people of faith died not yet having in hand what was promised, but still believing. How did they do it? They saw it way off in the distance, waved their greeting, and accepted the fact that they were transients in this world. People who live this way make it plain that they are looking for their true home. If they were homesick for the old country, they could have gone back any time they wanted. But they were after a far better country than that—heaven country. You can see why God is so proud of them, and has a City waiting for them.

Hebrews 11:1–3, 7–10, 13–16, THE MESSAGE

chapter twenty-seven
· · · · ·
Ready or Not —Here He Comes

My three boys share a bathroom. *Psycho* shower scene? That's mild compared to what three boys can do to a bathroom. Sopping towels, smoldering sweat socks—scary. The toilet paper in their bathroom is *never* on the roll. As a matter of fact, I think they consider it a bit of a toiletry perk when the roll sitting on the counter has soaked up its weight in cologne and assorted hair chemicals.

Environmental Disaster

I'm trying to be a good mom and train the boys to clean the bathroom themselves. I don't want their wives to hate me someday. So I've pretty much adopted a hands-off policy. Besides, last time I went in there I found a pile of those sweat socks decomposing. I've been wondering if I should start a compost pile.

When we're expecting company, however, I have to confess I adopt a completely new course of action. I put on my EPA-approved hazardous materials yellow suit and go in. But the other day unexpected company dropped by and managed to get to the boys' bathroom before I did (insert *Psycho* shower music here). I wanted to have them sign a release form, but they made it inside before I could tackle them. Ready or not, there they were. I didn't even have time to get the haz-mat suits.

Drop-in Company

God's Word says that Jesus is coming over, too—and he's not calling ahead. Will we be caught red-faced, digging for a release form, or expectantly and ecstatically prepared to meet him?

First John 2:28 (MSG) indicates there will be those who are caught off guard in the most embarrassing moment of all time. "Live deeply in Christ. Then we'll be ready for him when he appears, ready to receive him with open arms, with no cause for red-faced guilt or lame excuses when he arrives."

I want to be one of those caught "living deeply." His coming is a sure thing. First Thessalonians 4 (MSG) tells us, "We can tell you with complete confidence—we have the Master's word on it. ... The Master himself will give the command. Archangel thunder! God's trumpet blast! ... And then there will be one huge family reunion with the Master. So reassure one another with these words."

These words are only reassuring when there are no towels mildewing on the floor—when we're ready. When I hear the trumpet blast, I want to get a thrill from the music, not a *Psycho* shower/shriek reaction.

He's coming—ready or not. Let's get out the enviro-suits and finish the life cleaning so we don't have to be red-faced at his coming.

Equal Time for Girls

For the record, the bathroom disaster is not exclusively a guy thing. In all fairness to my boys, my two girls share a bathroom, too. Not only can the hairspray buildup on the floor rip the shoes right off your feet, but I'm afraid to ask how many electric hair tools one bathroom circuit can support. I wonder if the girls will be inspired to get it up to code if I tell them someone is coming.

And regarding the question, friends, that has come up about what happens to those already dead and buried, we don't want you in the dark any longer. First off, you must not carry on over them like people who have nothing to look forward to, as if the grave were the last word. Since Jesus died and broke loose from the grave, God will most certainly bring back to life those who died in Jesus.

And then this: We can tell you with complete confidence—we have the Master's word on it—that when the Master comes again to get us, those of us who are still alive will not get a jump on the dead and leave them behind. In actual fact, they'll be ahead of us. The Master himself will give the command. Archangel thunder! God's trumpet blast! He'll come down from heaven and the dead in Christ will rise—they'll go first. Then the rest of us who are still alive at the time will be caught up with them into the clouds to meet the Master. Oh, we'll be walking on air! And then there will be one huge family reunion with the Master. So reassure one another with these words.

I don't think, friends, that I need to deal with the question of when all this is going to happen. You know as well as I that the day of the Master's coming can't be posted on our calendars. He won't call ahead and make an appointment any more than a burglar would. About the time everybody's

walking around complacently, congratulating each other—
"We've sure got it made! Now we can take it easy!"—sud-
denly everything will fall apart. It's going to come as
suddenly and inescapably as birth pangs to a pregnant
woman.

But friends, you're not in the dark, so how could you be
taken off guard by any of this? You're sons of Light, daugh-
ters of Day. We live under wide open skies and know where
we stand. So let's not sleepwalk through life like those oth-
ers. Let's keep our eyes open and be smart.

1 Thessalonians 4:13–5:8, THE MESSAGE

chapter twenty-eight
· · · · ·
Living Large

I was speaking at a conference and had to rent a car to get from the airport to the conference site an hour or so away. I rented a real squirt of a car. The lady at the car rental desk asked if I'd like an upgrade. I answered, "Nah." After all, I'm only five feet tall. What would I do with extra leg room? I have no legs.

She handed me the keys and I made my way out to the lot. I found my numbered spot, but in the place where my little car-ette was supposed to be parked, sat the biggest Lincoln I've ever seen—a dinky car on major steroids. I wondered for a minute if the enormous thing had eaten my little car. Either someone had given me an unexpected upgrade or the car-ette had glandular problems like nobody's business.

Five-Star Car

The key worked, so I put my luggage into a trunk big enough to hold a revival meeting. I slid onto the leather seat and couldn't help but smile. Mind you, I'm used to my minivan at home. Not only are all the seats made of man-made, mega-processed, artificial materials, but most of those man-made materials are held together with half-eaten suckers. The mega car had leather. Leather! I was sitting on a car seat that used to be a cow. I snickered to myself, "Got car?"

My feet wouldn't reach the pedals, but the designers of the bus-mobile had evidently considered that. They didn't leave me dangling. No, they had a dozen buttons, knobs, and switches to adjust that seat almost to the next parking spot. There was an up button, down button, lumbar-support adjuster—over, across, under, and through buttons. I all but flattened myself against the car roof before I had it figured out.

After I got the seat adjusted, the control panel caught my eye. Lights, knobs, buttons, gauges—I think I could've ordered a cheeseburger with one of those switches. I felt like the captain of the starship *Enterprise*. I finally found the right controls to put it in gear. Engage warp engines.

Big Personalities

Even though I'm a short person, I had a big reaction to a big car—and I had big fun! If you've ever studied the temperaments, you may have noticed that we of the Sanguine persuasion do everything big. We like to enter a room big. We're happy big. We're sad big. Everything is BIG.

As a person with a rather big personality (though I like to think of it as merely "thick boned"), I've noticed I can also sin big. I can pout big. I can blame big. I can show you selfishness in its biggest form. I'm so thankful for God's abundant grace that's always infinitely bigger.

Our God Is a BIG God

The funny thing was that when I rented the car, I asked "small." I got big. Isn't that how God often responds to us? Even though our faith may be small and our sin disproportionately big, his love, grace, and forgiveness are even bigger.

Praise God, he does everything big. We can't out sin his grace. And he gives abundant life to replace the abundant sin. Romans 5:20 (TLB) says, "The Ten Commandments were given so that all could see the extent of their failure to obey God's laws. But the more we see our sinfulness, the more we see God's abounding grace forgiving us."

You gotta love an abounding grace! First Timothy 1:14 (NKJV) tells us again: "And the grace of our Lord was exceedingly abundant, with faith and love which are in Christ Jesus." Psalm 86:15 (NKJV) reminds us that he's big in mercy, grace, and truth, but also hugely patient: "But You, O Lord, are a God full of compassion, and gracious, longsuffering and abundant in mercy and truth."

What's Our Part?

Isaiah 55:6–7 (TLB) says to "Seek the Lord while you can find him. Call upon him now while he is near. Let men cast off their wicked deeds; let them banish from their minds the very thought of doing wrong! Let them turn to the Lord that he may have mercy upon them, and to our God, for he will abundantly pardon!" How big is abundant pardon? As big as we need it to be!

Psalm 86:5 (HCSB) reminds us of his abundant forgiveness and mercy. "For You, Lord, are kind and ready to forgive, abundant in faithful love to all who call on you."

Both passages remind us of our part. Our part is to "seek" the Lord and to "call" on him.

Living Large

God forgives big. He loves big. He is big. And he gives us life in the biggest way. It's a turbocharged life with every option added in. Jesus said, "I have come that they may have life, and that they may have it more abundantly" (John 10:10, NKJV).

As we live in his big love, we learn that we can trust him in the biggest way. We learn we can ask as big as we can think—bigger—and he loves to answer. "Now to Him who is able to do exceedingly abundantly above all that we ask or think, according to the power that works in us, to Him be glory…" (Eph. 3:20–21 NKJV). He loves to answer BIG.

I wonder what would've happened if I had prayed "big" at the car rental place? Would I have gotten a TANK?

They will celebrate your abundant goodness and joyfully sing of your righteousness. The LORD is gracious and compassionate, slow to anger and rich in love. The LORD is good to all; he has compassion on all he has made. All you have made will praise you, O LORD; your saints will extol you. They will tell of the glory of your kingdom and speak of your might, so that all men may know of your mighty acts and the glorious splendor of your kingdom. Your kingdom is an everlasting kingdom, and your dominion endures through all generations. The LORD is faithful to all his promises and loving toward all he has made.

Psalm 145:7–13

chapter twenty-nine
· · · · ·
Mount Launder-more

There's always a mountain of laundry at my house. With five kids, ours is more of a series of mountain ranges: not only Mount Launder-more, but also Mount Wash-it-tomorrow, which trails right into Mount Never-rest.

The kids help by taking care of most of their own things, but I can't even count how many times we've washed a handful of tissues. Washing non-laundry items is a normal happening, too—things like ink pens. I hate when it's a permanent marker. I really hate when it's a pack of Juicy Fruit. And I really, really hate when it's real fruit. Can anyone tell me how half a dozen apples got into the wash? And how did the kids manage to miss all of them when they put that load into the dryer? Maybe it was their attempt to make their own dried fruit. I won't even tell you what happened with the cantaloupe. But let me just say that if you've ever had someone put a cantaloupe in your dryer, even on the gentle cycle, it doesn't take long to figure out something weird is happening. Bowling for laundry! It's like discovering one of the mountains is actually an explosively active volcano. Major laundry-quake.

Change of Clothes

At least we don't ever have to buy fireworks. Every two or three days a pair of jeans gets dumped into the dryer with a couple of pockets full of gravel. It sounds like a Chinese New Year celebration. It's a little embarrassing when the kids start a load of laundry when we have company, though. Last time two or three guests ended up dashing for cover—right under the table.

If you manage to make it past the washing and drying cycles without incident (I think it's happened to me twice), there's still the hanging, folding, and putting away to gum up the system—yes, even without the Juicy Fruit. Does anyone else have as much trouble getting it all hung up as I do? Why can't we simply hang the clothes right on the kids? Just asking the questions makes me a little tired. It's Mount Neverrest, all right.

Laundry by the Peace

But in the Lord we can find real rest. Sort of an anti-laundry situation, if you will. Not "Never rest," but "Ever rest." In Psalm 62:1–2 David reminds us where to go when we're tired: "My soul finds rest in God alone; my salvation comes from him. He alone is my rock and my salvation; he is my fortress, I will never be shaken."

Just as if we were scooped up in a giant laundry basket, we're carried by our Father when we learn to trust and rest in him. Psalm 68:19–20 (MSG) says, "Blessed be the Lord—day after day he carries us along. He's our Savior, our God, oh yes! He's God-for-us, he's God-who-saves-us." How wonderful to be carried by the God Most High! He's all-powerful—and higher than any mountain. Even higher than Mount Wash-more.

Head for the Mountains

In Christ we're given a rest that doesn't depend on circumstances, laundry or otherwise. It's an unexplainable peace that blankets even our biggest trials (and this blanket never causes problems in the lint filter). Want to be blanketed with his peace? Run to him. He's asking you to "Come to me, all you who are weary and burdened, and I will give you rest. Take my yoke upon you and learn from me, for I am gentle and humble in heart, and you will find rest for your souls. For my yoke is easy and my burden is light" (Matt. 11:28–30). He lightens every burden—more than that, he carries every burden. Let him become your Mount Ever-rest!

As for the other mountains, my husband couldn't figure out why I had to shudder just a little when he mentioned vacationing in the mountains. I guess it was because it seemed to be a bit of an oxymoron in laundry language—especially when he mentioned that fresh mountain air. April fresh.

For the LORD is the great God, the great King above all gods. In his hand are the depths of the earth, and the mountain peaks belong to him. The sea is his, for he made it, and his hands formed the dry land. Come, let us bow down in worship, let us kneel before the LORD our Maker; for he is our God and we are the people of his pasture, the flock under his care. Today, if you hear his voice, do not harden your hearts as you did at Meribah, as you did that day at Massah in the desert, where your fathers tested and tried me, though they had seen what I did. For forty years I was angry with that generation; I said, "They are a people whose hearts go astray, and they have not known my ways." So I declared on oath in my anger, "They shall never enter my rest."

Psalm 95:3–11

chapter thirty
· · · · ·
New and Improved

I remember our first brand-new car. I can almost smell that wonderful new-car smell. It's a pretty distant memory, of course. If the new car is a *family* car, the new smell lasts about twenty minutes, depending on exactly when the kids are allowed in. My car now smells like kid sweat and week-old burgers. I once found a French fry in one of the cup holders that looked like a little string of yarn. A little string of *blue* yarn. And here's an interesting factoid: Did you know that if you leave a cup of grape drink in the car long enough, it will achieve status as a life form? It's probably protected under some kind of government provision. At least we were able to claim a couple of extra dependents on our tax return.

Still, that wonderful new-car smell is filed away in a special place in my memory. It's filed far, far away—but it's there nonetheless.

Nosing Around at Home
There's another new smell in the brain file cabinet. Not long ago we built a new home. I can still catch a whiff of that new-house smell now and then, though I have to confess, it tends to compete with petrifying

towels from the kids' bathrooms and a few containers of who-knows-what growing in the fridge.

I just bought a new pair of shoes, too. Okay, those I didn't sniff. Maybe they have that new-shoe smell, I don't know. But there's something about a new pair that gives me a little new-shoe rush.

Let's Be Scents-ible

As great as all those new things are, there's another type of newness that's eternally more exciting. Our heavenly Father can take the stench of our sin (infinitely worse than anything I have growing in my car) and change it into something downright aromatic. He makes us brand, spanking new! Second Corinthians 5:17 reminds us what Christ has done for us: "Therefore, if anyone is in Christ, he is a new creation; the old has gone, the new has come!"

Out with the Old, In with the New

Merely trying to cover over sin with good deeds is like trying to mask a month's worth of fast-food burgers by hanging a four-inch, paper evergreen tree on the rearview mirror. Talk about futile! In Luke 5:36–39, Jesus told this parable: "No one tears a patch from a new garment and sews it on an old one. If he does, he will have torn the new garment, and the patch from the new will not match the old. And no one pours new wine into old wineskins. If he does, the new wine will burst the skins, the wine will run out and the wineskins will be ruined. No, new wine must be poured into new wineskins. And no one after drinking old wine wants the new, for he says, 'The old is better.'"

We have to deal with the sin—get rid of it—not try to mask it with cheap air fresheners. "You were taught, with regard to your former way of life, to put off your old self, which is being corrupted by its deceitful desires; to be made new in the attitude of your minds; and to put on the new self, created to be like God in true righteousness and holiness" (Eph. 4:22–24).

Put off the old self. Get rid of it. Let it die. Romans 6:4 tells us, "We were therefore buried with him through baptism into death in order that, just as Christ was raised from the dead through the glory of the Father, we too may live a new life."

If there were any such thing as a "new-self" smell, it would far surpass the new-car and the new-house smells put together!

Sniff This

Judge others by smell? Okay, that's a weird thought. But we're often tempted to judge others in weird ways—how they look, what they own, and lots of other things that don't tell us a thing about what's happening in their hearts and minds. Every person, blue yarn or no blue yarn, has the same opportunity for newness in Christ.

> Our firm decision is to work from this focused center: One man died for everyone. That puts everyone in the same boat. He included everyone in his death so that everyone could also be included in his life, a resurrection life, a far better life than people ever lived on their own.
>
> Because of this decision we don't evaluate people by what they have or how they look. We looked at the Messiah that way once and got it all wrong, as you know. We certainly don't look at him that way anymore. Now we look inside, and what we see is that anyone united with the Messiah gets a fresh start, is created new. The

old life is gone; a new life burgeons! Look at it! All this comes from the God who settled the relationship between us and him, and then called us to settle our relationships with each other. God put the world square with himself through the Messiah, giving the world a fresh start by offering forgiveness of sins. God has given us the task of telling everyone what he is doing. We're Christ's representatives. God uses us to persuade men and women to drop their differences and enter into God's work of making things right between them. We're speaking for Christ himself now: Become friends with God; he's already a friend with you.

"How?" you say. In Christ. God put the wrong on him who never did anything wrong, so we could be put right with God. (2 Cor. 5:14–21 MSG)

Brand-new life is available to us all. It's here and now, and it's our eternal future. Revelation 21:5 tells us, "He who was seated on the throne said, 'I am making everything new!' Then he said, 'Write this down, for these words are trustworthy and true.'"

And through new life in Christ, life—past, present, and always—is good! New and improved! No matter what's growing in the cup holder.

What a God we have! And how fortunate we are to have him, this Father of our Master Jesus! Because Jesus was raised from the dead, we've been given a brand-new life and have everything to live for, including a future in heaven—and the future starts now! God is keeping careful watch over us and the future. The Day is coming when you'll have it all—life healed and whole.

I know how great this makes you feel, even though you have to put up with every kind of aggravation in the meantime. Pure gold put in the fire comes out of it proved pure; genuine faith put through this suffering comes out proved genuine. When Jesus wraps this all up, it's your faith, not your gold, that God will have on display as evidence of his victory.

1 Peter 1:3–7, THE MESSAGE

part seven

What Are You Serving?

Serving and Teaching the Family to Serve

chapter thirty-one

· · · · ·
Family Feud

Every once in awhile we have a week when I feel like I'm living in Wedgie-ville. Daniel is the youngest of five kids, and because of this, most of his underwear has no waistband. Daniel-wedgies are a common form of entertainment among the older Rhea kids. They used to be able to administer eyeball-popping wedgies before poor Daniel even saw them coming. But the constant wedgie-blitzes seem to be honing his reflexes more and more all the time. He's had a great soccer season, and I really have to give some of the credit to his older sibs. I don't think he'll ever need to take karate. He's already gone way past "wax on, wax off" to "waistband on, waistband off."

Wedgie-ville is conveniently located right next to Noogie City. Among all the wedgies, there are many headlocks waiting to be secured. Oh, the demanding schedule of a preadolescent with older siblings. Daniel once asked me with a grin if I thought he would be able to sue someday.

Family Sued

You might be happy to know that we always step in somewhere before the need for litigation. As persistent as the wedgie-givers can be, we parents can be even more persistent. We're constantly working to teach all those little Rhea-lings to serve each other unselfishly. Yes, I've sensed a few eye rolls now and then (though none of them would dare roll when we're looking). But we really do see a little more selflessness every day. It's fun watching them mature. I'd say in a dozen or so years Daniel should have no wedgie-worries whatsoever. Of course, he'll be in his twenties by then.

I couldn't find a specific de-wedgie-ing verse in the Bible, but Ephesians 6:7 tells us to "Serve wholeheartedly, as if you were serving the Lord, not men." It reminds me to stay on my toes in my own service— heart and soul—and to teach my kids to serve with everything they have, too.

Family Pewed

One way I can keep up the anti-wedgie/noogie training is by making sure my kids are planted in the pews of a solidly serving, Bible-believing church each week. Our kids will learn more about service and will see more servants in action as we parents stay consistent in church attendance. If you're not involved in the kind of church you and your kids need, don't weary of searching one out. Let the church help you pour biblical truths for living into the lives and hearts of your children. It's a great place for your teaching to be reinforced. The church was created by God's design, and he wants us to be a part of it. He spells it out for us in Hebrews 10:25 (MSG): "Let's see how inventive we can be in encouraging love and helping out, not avoiding worshiping together as some do but spurring each other on, especially as we see the big Day approaching."

Romans 15:17–18 tells us that our service is something

we can treasure in life—because anything good in our lives happens as a result of letting Jesus work in and through us. "Therefore I glory in Christ Jesus in my service to God. I will not venture to speak of anything except what Christ has accomplished through me in leading the Gentiles to obey God by what I have said and done." Is there anything that tickles parents more than seeing their kids allowing the Lord to grow them up in their service for him?

As always, we need to do more than just tell our children to be servants. They need to be able to learn it by our example. We're being good examples and we're being obedient to the Lord when we lovingly serve. Galatians 5:13 tells us to "serve one another in love."

Family Cued

I want my family to stay right on cue with what the Lord wants for us. I'll mention again that when Jesus comes for us, I hope we're all caught red-handed in selfless, loving service. He gives us some readying instructions:

> Be dressed ready for service and keep your lamps burning, like men waiting for their master to return from a wedding banquet, so that when he comes and knocks they can immediately open the door for him. It will be good for those servants whose master finds them watching when he comes. I tell you the truth, he will dress himself to serve, will have them recline at the table and will come and wait on them. It will be good for those servants whose master finds them ready, even if he comes in the second or third watch of the night. But understand this: If the owner of the house had known at what hour the thief was

coming, he would not have let his house be broken into. You also must be ready, because the Son of Man will come at an hour when you do not expect him. (Luke 12:35–40)

As a mother, I would say being dressed and ready would include wearing clean underwear—the kind with a waistband that's still intact. But what does Jesus consider "all dressed up and ready to go" according to this passage? Serving! "Be dressed ready for service," he said! The "big Day" is approaching!

Let's help our children be ready for Jesus' coming by dressing for service. We can stick together and become more like a "family glued."

You, my brothers, were called to be free. But do not use your freedom to indulge the sinful nature; rather, serve one another in love. The entire law is summed up in a single command: "Love your neighbor as yourself." If you keep on biting and devouring each other, watch out or you will be destroyed by each other.

Galatians 5:13–15

chapter thirty-two
Dishing It Out

Ugh, I've had a cold bug this week. Or could this be a brain infection? How is it that a germ smaller than I can see has the ability to drop me like a bag of dirt? Don't you just hate the thought of microscopic critters creeping into your body and wreaking havoc?

And exactly what number does an at-home mom phone when she needs to call in sick? Where do moms call in brain-dead? If I had an office to call, I'm sure I would've had to call in comatose. But, alas, no number to call, no clock to punch. Home life goes on. I've noticed, however, that it goes on in a totally different manner when the mom is out of commission. Any remote sense of order that I'd been hanging on to (and I confess, it was remote) went totally out the window.

"Don't worry, Mom. We'll take care of our own dinner. Oh yeah, is there a difference between 'broil' and 'bake'?" That dinner really did have to be thrown out the window. Fortunately it missed the deck and only scorched the grass.

By the way, it doesn't matter how many times you ask the family to let you rest undisturbed for a few hours so you can get better. It just doesn't happen. Too many "emergencies" require a woman's input. "Mom, where are my soccer socks?" "Honey, do you remember what check number 4723 was for?" And, my personal favorite: "Mom, what should I use to get blood out of the carpet? I've got Pledge or Windex." That one always gets my attention—in oh, so many ways.

Ready to Unload

Just as I was about ready to go slightly ballistic, I got a little surprise. I went into the kitchen and looked around at the devastation (I guess sort of the way people stop to look at a train wreck). The critters of the non-microscopic persuasion had been wreaking their havoc, too.

Then I saw the kids taking glasses out of the dishwasher. That doesn't sound all that unusual, except each of them then took another. And another. How thirsty were these kids? Then it hit me: *They're unloading the dishwasher.* And I hadn't asked them to! I accidentally swallowed my throat lozenge whole.

I wonder if that's how God feels when we serve him— not because we're in the middle of some kind of peril, not even out of duty, but when we serve simply out of love for him. It must make him "lozenge-swallowing" proud. In Deuteronomy 10:12 the Israelites were getting their "stepping into the Promised Land" instructions: "And now, O Israel, what does the LORD your God ask of you but to fear the LORD your God, to walk in all his ways, to love him, to serve the LORD your God with all your heart and with all your soul."

Heart and Soul

Serving "with heart and soul" is serving out of love. It's a loving service that also calls us to obedience. Verse 13 says "and to observe the LORD's commands and decrees that I am giving you today for your own good."

Lovingly serving the Lord really does turn out for our own good. That's not why we should do it, but it doesn't hurt to remember that doing things God's way sets in motion natural consequences he has put in place. Of course, doing things contrary to God's way sets in motion some natural consequences, too. Those are not pretty.

Service with a Smile

I want to teach my kids the right kind of service—germ invasion or no germ invasion. I want them to know how to serve even more than I want them to know how to use Pledge and/or Windex—although I have to admit that when my son asked me that question, I responded with "Put down the cleaners and slowly step away from my carpet." Don't worry, I remembered to ask if there were any immediate tourniquet needs—and I'm pretty sure I asked that before I asked about the carpet.

As scary as it is sometimes, I know that the best way to teach them is by my example of putting others' needs ahead of my own, even when I feel crummy. Despite my assorted comas, my children need to see me lovingly, selflessly, obediently serving. Conviction—ouch.

O Lord, let that be the kind of service I consistently "dish out"!

So now Israel, what do you think GOD expects from you? Just this: Live in his presence in holy reverence, follow the road he sets out for you, love him, serve GOD, your GOD, with everything you have in you, obey the commandments and regulations of GOD *that I'm commanding you today—live a good life.*

Look around you: Everything you see is GOD's—*the heavens above and beyond, the Earth, and everything on it. But it was your ancestors that* GOD *fell in love with; he picked their children—that's you!—out of all the other peoples. That's where we are right now. So cut away the thick calluses from your heart and stop being so willfully hardheaded.* GOD, *your* GOD, *is the God of all gods, he's the Master of all masters, a God immense and powerful and awesome.*

Deuteronomy 10:12–17, THE MESSAGE

chapter thirty-three

Kid Threats

The older my kids get, the more changes I have to make in the way I threaten them (and I'm using the term "threaten" in its purest, most well-meaning, spiritually mature way). I guess eventually the only good threat I'll have left will be "Do you want me to strike you from the will?" Still, a good old threat of grounding seems to be timeless. Surely it has the power to send chills down the spines of kids of all ages. I think my mom could still scare *me* with that one.

Of course, we parents keep quite a reserve of staple threats: "Never run with scissors—you'll put an eye out"; "If you don't clean your ears, potatoes are going to grow in there"; "Eat your vegetables or children in poor countries are going to starve"; "Don't cross your eyes or they'll get stuck like that"; "Don't swallow those seeds or watermelons will grow out your ears."

That watermelon threat traumatized me as a child. I accidentally swallowed a seed and was just sure I was going to end up having to weed-whack my head. The potato one didn't really worry me. It was just too weird to believe. Besides, I had a Mr. Potato Head and he seemed happy.

Sealed with a Name

All good kid threats are sealed with a kid's full name. Want oomph in your threats? Add the first, middle, and last name combo. It always put the fear of God in me when I was a kid.

Why does the threat of grounding work? I guess it's because we hate to be told we can't do something we want to do. We hate to be told we have to do something we don't want to do, too.

Get Running!

When we find instructions in God's Word that tell us what we're supposed to be doing, we need to sit up and take notice. It's like God calling us by our first, middle, and last names. Paul said in Ephesians 4:1–3 (MSG), "In light of all this, here's what I want you to do." This is his "here's what I want you to do," full-name call to take notice. "While I'm locked up here, a prisoner for the Master, I want you to get out there and walk—better yet, run!—on the road God called you to travel. I don't want any of you sitting around on your hands. I don't want anyone strolling off, down some path that goes nowhere. And mark that you do this with humility and discipline—not in fits and starts, but steadily, pouring yourselves out for each other in acts of love, alert at noticing differences and quick at mending fences."

No lazy-bones, potato-growing stuff! We've been called to walk—even run—in selfless service. We're called to pour ourselves out for our families, for others—for Christ! And would you like a truly grand surprise? The life of service is a life of joy! It's not punishment.

To be honest, it's not always necessarily easy either. But when we stay alert in our service for Christ, there are great rewards, here and in the hereafter. Galatians 6:7–10 (MSG) says,

Don't be misled: No one makes a fool of God. What a person plants, he will harvest. The person who plants selfishness, ignoring the needs of others—ignoring God!—harvests a crop of weeds. All he'll have to show for his life is weeds! But the one who plants in response to God, letting God's Spirit do the growth work in him, harvests a crop of real life, eternal life. So let's not allow ourselves to get fatigued doing good. At the right time we will harvest a good crop if we don't give up, or quit. Right now, therefore, every time we get the chance, let us work for the benefit of all, starting with the people closest to us in the community of faith.

Keep It Going

Hebrews 6:10–12 (MSG) tells us that God notices when we keep on serving: "He knows perfectly well all the love you've shown him by helping needy Christians, and that you keep at it. And now I want each of you to extend that same intensity toward a full-bodied hope, and keep at it till the finish. Don't drag your feet. Be like those who stay the course with committed faith and then get everything promised to them."

If we don't drag our feet, we'll live a blessed life and be a blessing and a witness to everyone who sees us—inside and outside the family. Paul gave instructions in 1 Timothy 4 to keep it up—keep on using our gifts in service! Then he said to "Cultivate these things. Immerse yourself in them. The people will all see you mature right before their eyes! Keep a firm grasp on both your character and your teaching. Don't be diverted. Just keep at it. Both you and those who hear you will experience salvation" (vv. 14–16 MSG).

Maturity—what a great bonus. Not only will we become more mature—it will happen right out there for everyone to see! Keep in mind what an impact your service will have on your life, your family, and on all those around you.

And if you're resorting to threats, you might want to also keep in mind the ultimate parent threat. It's a classic: "I hope someday you have a kid just like you. No, make it two."

And the special gift of ministry you received when I laid hands on you and prayed—keep that ablaze! God doesn't want us to be shy with his gifts, but bold and loving and sensible. So don't be embarrassed to speak up for our Master or for me, his prisoner. Take your share of suffering for the Message along with the rest of us. We can only keep on going, after all, by the power of God, who first saved us and then called us to this holy work.

2 Timothy 1:6–9, THE MESSAGE

chapter thirty-four
· · · · ·
Who Put the Cat in the Refrigerator?

I've wondered if I should put a revolving door on our refrigerator. It's forever swinging open, closed, open, closed. You should watch its gyratory action each morning. Andrew opens it to drink almost half a gallon of milk—out of the carton. He thinks I don't see. What he doesn't know is I'm just happy he puts it back in the fridge when he's done. Then Jordan opens the door to take out a quarter of a cold pizza—yes, for breakfast. Kaley comes back for the milk, not realizing Andrew drank out of the carton. I'm not telling her. Allie swings the door open looking for whatever it is we happen to be out of. Then Daniel opens it up and just stares blankly. He eats the same thing every morning, but he has to stare into the fridge for a good five minutes first. Then he eats cereal. The milk is still out and the cereal is in the pantry. What is he looking for?

Cool Cat

One morning while the fridge door swiveled in its

orbit, I worked my way into the line to get some butter. I swung open the door and got a humongous shock. A cat jumped out! It's a good thing that door is never shut for more than a few seconds in the morning or we could've opened it later to find a kitty-cicle. What was that crazy cat thinking?

Granted, there are goodies in the fridge that would be considered fancy fare to this cat. The cat was a new addition; we'd taken her in recently when she got dumped at church. We called her Sunday because it sounded right for a church cat. But she was one pitifully scrawny feline. Still, sneaking into the refrigerator? Do you suppose she knew how close she came to taking a permanent catnap? There's a cat willing to completely give its all for a chicken leg! I mean *give all*!

Giving All

Every once in awhile, I have to ask myself if I'm really willing to completely give all—to sacrifice my comfort, my warmth, whatever I might be tempted to hang on to.

I'm often amazed that God doesn't simply demand our all. He certainly has every right to. He made us. Then he redeemed us back to himself through the death of his Son. He has all rights of ownership. But instead of demanding our all, he asks us to offer ourselves.

Abraham gave us a good example of offering all. He offered Isaac with no strings attached. That's the kind of offering God desires—complete, nothing held back. Ninety-nine point nine percent on the altar won't cut it. What if Abraham had said, "Listen God, I'll give you some of Isaac—how about the fingernails?" That wouldn't have been a complete offering, would it? It wouldn't really have been an offering at all. Or what if Abraham had said, "Okay, God, I'll make this sacrifice, but I'm keeping a lock of hair so I'll at least hang on to something of him"?

Hanging on does not result in a real offering. A complete offering is a hands-off presentation, and it's the result of complete trust.

Sweet Surrender

Obedience, giving all, sacrificing, trusting—they all go together. They call for surrender of self, surrender to Christ. Surrender is agreeing to serve—giving all in complete abandon—before we even know how he wants us to serve. Here's the kicker: agreeing to serve is not disagreeable. It's glorious!

In his book *The Purpose-Driven Life®*, Rick Warren wrote that "God is not a cruel slave driver or a bully who uses brute force to coerce us into submission. He doesn't try to break our will, but woos us to himself so that we might offer ourselves freely to him. God is a lover and a liberator, and surrendering to him brings freedom, not bondage. When we completely surrender ourselves to Jesus, we discover that he is not a tyrant, but a savior; not a boss, but a brother; not a dictator, but a friend."[1]

What an honor it is to become a friend of God. Jesus made it happen. He said in John 15:14–15, "You are my friends if you do what I command. I no longer call you servants, because a servant does not know his master's business. Instead, I have called you friends, for everything that I learned from my Father I have made known to you."

The Best of Friends

And what happened to Abraham when he was willing to give all? He became known as a "friend of God."

James 2:21–23 reminds us, "Was not our ancestor Abraham considered righteous for what he did when he offered his son Isaac on the altar? You see that his faith and his actions were working together, and his faith was made complete by what he did. And the scripture was fulfilled that says, 'Abraham believed God, and it was credited to him as righteousness,' and he was called God's friend."

There's no better friend than the Lord God. He is the only one worthy of our complete trust and obedience—our all. So let's not be caught catnapping. Doors of opportunity for service are forever swinging open. Come to think of it, that really is a lot like my fridge.

"But you, O Israel, my servant, Jacob, whom I have chosen, you descendants of Abraham my friend, I took you from the ends of the earth, from its farthest corners I called you. I said, 'You are my servant'; I have chosen you and have not rejected you. So do not fear, for I am with you; do not be dismayed, for I am your God. I will strengthen you and help you; I will uphold you with my righteous right hand. All who rage against you will surely be ashamed and disgraced; those who oppose you will be as nothing and perish. Though you search for your enemies, you will not find them. Those who wage war against you will be as nothing at all. For I am the LORD, your God, who takes hold of your right hand and says to you, Do not fear; I will help you."

Isaiah 41:8–13

chapter thirty-five
· · · · ·
King of
the Jungle

'Twas the night before the Christmas party
And all through the house
Every person was stirring
And I ruined my good blouse ...

Instead of one of those special, Norman Rockwell–type moments, family members dashed all over the house, each of us involved in the four "C's" of that particular Rhea Christmas party: cooking, crabbing, cleaning, and complaining.

Somebody, Give Me a Hand!

I had one hand in dishwater scrubbing pots and pans, one hand in an oven mitt hoisting cookies out of the oven, and one hand trying to fish anything rotten out of the fridge (the three-handed mom has always been quite the novel sight). Everything needed to be done at once, and I couldn't find my children. If I'd had a spare hand, I'd have pulled out my hair.

My children are pretty talented at disappearing when there's chaos to clear. I, however, am the Great Hunter. A little sniff in the air told me that someone's socks had been dropped in the kitchen. Then I found a book bag that had been dropped in the family room. Candy wrappers had been dropped near the TV. Yes, I can always trail my kids. Like all good trackers, I just follow the droppings.

When Did We Become Tarzan and Jane?

What is this, a house or a jungle? Two of the kids tracked me down (that kind of switch up is rarely good news). They wanted to tell me their toilet had overflowed. I fought off the urge to mumble, "Oom-gah-wah," and asked instead, "Did you tell your dad?" He always knows how to swing to the rescue in those kinds of jungle dangers. He's not exactly a vine-swinger, but the man swings a mean plunger.

While he dealt with the toilet (you can picture Tarzan battling a crocodile), I dealt with wild animals in the fridge. I thought I heard a shriek coming from a container of what used to be corn. The lid was stuck, or maybe the corn was holding it on, I'm not sure which. I gave it a yank and watched in horror as the putrid corn-type creature leaped toward me. I swatted wildly and I think I killed it, but its remains were all over my Christmas party outfit. Before I could stop myself, I let out a yell that brought my husband running. Hey, maybe I *was* Jane!

I changed clothes and before we knew it, it was time to take care of a kajillion last-minute tasks: set all the food out, hide everything that's still out that's not supposed to be, and, one more time, recite the poetic reminder to the kids to "floss, brush, and for heaven's sake, flush."

It's Party Time!

The party was a blast—not because the house was in

order, or the food perfect—certainly not because the refrigerator was spotless (I know that for a fact, since I was afraid to go back and finish it after the terrifying corn incident). Know what made it a great party? It was the people. Somewhere in the hubbub, I really should've stopped to remind my kids—and myself— that we wanted our guests to feel at home in this place, not make our home into a showplace. It's not about me—it's about ministry.

Raising Hospitable Kids

I want to raise kids who know how to be hospitable. I want them to be able to learn by my teaching and by my example. I want to cut the complaining (and prefer- ably the corn). First Peter 4:9 tells us to "Offer hospi- tality to one another without grumbling." Ouch.

I want my kids to learn to hold their "things" loosely and in a non-grumbly fashion. Anytime we have an open house, I remind them that we emphasize the "open" part. Every place is accessible—including their rooms. (If, however, any guest takes the outrageous risk of looking in a closet, I try to make sure they release us from liability for any subsequent therapy they might need. But then, that's just me.) Teaching our kids to release their things, to give sacrificially, to think of others, and to become unselfish givers is at the heart of being a good teacher.

Romans 12:10–16 gives some great party training for all of us: "Be devoted to one another in brotherly love. Honor one another above yourselves. Never be lacking in zeal, but keep your spiritual fervor, serving the Lord. Be joyful in hope, patient in affliction, faith- ful in prayer. Share with God's people who are in need. Practice hospitality. Bless those who persecute you; bless and do not curse. Rejoice with those who rejoice;

mourn with those who mourn. Live in harmony with one another. Do not be proud, but be willing to associate with people of low position. Do not be conceited."

When it says to "practice" hospitality, do you suppose that means we need to keep rehearsing it until we're good at it? I'm willing to give it a try—in any and all wild jungle situations.

King of the Jungle

The bottom line is that Jesus needs to be King of all: King of our time, King of our home, King of our parties, King of our work, King of our rest, King of our *jungle*.

And since Romans 12:13 (MSG) tells us to "...be inventive in hospitality," I think for the entertainment portion of our next party, I just might pull out the corn number.

Above all, love each other deeply, because love covers over a multitude of sins. Offer hospitality to one another without grumbling. Each one should use whatever gift he has received to serve others, faithfully administering God's grace in its various forms. If anyone speaks, he should do it as one speaking the very words of God. If anyone serves, he should do it with the strength God provides, so that in all things God may be praised through Jesus Christ. To him be the glory and the power for ever and ever. Amen.

1 Peter 4:8–11

part eight

Love-covered Hearts with Happy-cream Filling

Loving Wholeheartedly

chapter thirty-six
· · · · ·
Mom-zilla

hy do the little things always set me off? It was Valentine's Day—the day we're supposed to be celebrating love—but I didn't feel all lovey-dovey, ooey-gooey. I felt more frumpy-grumpy, slouchy-grouchy. I guess because there had been more than just one or two of those "little things" working to set me off. There'd been a string of the suckers stretching from here to Montana.

I was off to a bad start when the outfit I wanted to wear suddenly shrank about a size and a half. I was sure someone had been sneaking into my closet and washing all my clothes in hot water. Dastardly. It made me crave Valentine chocolates. On top of that, I'd been trying all day to get the house picked up so I could have a relatively guilt-free date with my favorite Valentine. But the kids didn't cooperate. I got the family room picked up, then noticed the next time I went through that someone had dumped out the box of crayons (you know, the giant shoebox where we keep generations of crayon crumbs, plus the paper that used to be wrapped around them).

I finally got the kitchen cleaned, only to pass through a few minutes later and find someone had fixed a bologna sandwich. The bread was out—and open. The bologna was out—and the cat was staring at it with great interest. The mayonnaise was out, too—though I'd say more of it was smeared on the counter than left in the bottle.

Running on Fumes

I don't know why I move so much faster when I'm fuming. Maybe I should work up a good fury every time I clean. I'd get it all done in less than half the time. Anyway, as I dashed across the kitchen in fume mode, I ran into the open dishwasher door. Though my kids are not necessarily known for using the dishwasher for its original purpose, I've noticed they often help me use it as an effective shin-finding device. I don't know how I managed to smash both shins on the thing, but I did. I leaned on the counter, holding my breath, and wondered how many lovely colors my shins would be sporting the next few weeks. At least they'd match.

When I finally let out the breath I was holding, it came out as a bellow to my kids: "Newsflash, people! This place is a disaster again!"

I heard one of them whisper, "Film at eleven."

That did it. I had an off-the-cuff lecture—and I knew how to use it. I brought up everything they had done that they weren't supposed to, and everything they hadn't done that they were supposed to have done. I pointed out a fault here and threw in a scolding there—and then a few solid nags just for good measure. I may have even accused them of viciously laundering my clothes—I'm not exactly sure. I finished it off with, "Why don't I just give each one of you a chili dog and a glass of cherry soda and sit you on my off-white sofa?" Valentine love filled the air.

Loving With Oomph

Richie and I eventually got our Valentine date that night, but I was spent. I'd put a lot of energy into building a nice little celebration. I'd put out loads of energy trying to get my house in order. I had put even more energy behind the delivery of my surly speech. But as things settled down and I thought about the day, I realized I hadn't put much energy into making it a real day of love around the house. What a waste of energy.

Romans 14:19 (MSG) says, "So let's agree to use all our energy in getting along with each other. Help others with encouraging words; don't drag them down by finding fault." Some days, building love requires more than a little energy. It requires all of it. But then, dragging people down by finding fault is a real energy drain, too.

I want to do a better job of spending my energies wisely. If respecting my children with words of love requires the same energy as dissing them, why diss? "Make a clean break with all cutting, backbiting, profane talk," we're told in Ephesians 4:31 (MSG). Even when we're stressed, we can guard our words. First Thessalonians 5:14 (MSG) gives us these instructions: "And be careful that when you get on each other's nerves you don't snap at each other. Look for the best in each other, and always do your best to bring it out."

Even words of discipline can be delivered with love and respect with just the right battery power invested. Where can I find the power? I can find it when I stay plugged in to the love of Jesus. In John 15:9, Jesus said, "Now remain in my love." Remain in—stay connected to—his love.

Colorful Love

Jesus was serious about love. He made it a command

in John 13:34–35: "A new command I give you: Love one another. As I have loved you, so you must love one another. By this all men will know that you are my disciples, if you love one another." He certainly didn't command us to do anything he wasn't willing to do himself. He instructs us to love the way he loves us. Christ loves to the max. He loved all the way to the cross. When we love with his kind of sacrificial love, everyone we encounter will understand what a difference he makes in our lives. They'll know we're his disciples—even at every dishwasher door encounter.

Do I have to admit how little I look like a disciple when I'm nagging my children? Mayonnaise messes and crayon clutter really are "little things." I want to spend my energy becoming the "disciple-like" mom, not the monster one. The Mom-zilla look is just not the look for me—though you might not readily know that if you could see the color of these shins.

"As the Father has loved me, so have I loved you. Now remain in my love. If you obey my commands, you will remain in my love, just as I have obeyed my Father's commands and remain in his love. I have told you this so that my joy may be in you and that your joy may be complete. My command is this: Love each other as I have loved you. Greater love has no one than this, that he lay down his life for his friends. You are my friends if you do what I command. I no longer call you servants, because a servant does not know his master's business. Instead, I have called you friends, for everything that I learned from my Father I have made known to you. You did not choose me, but I chose you and appointed you to go and bear fruit—fruit that will last. Then the Father will give you whatever you ask in my name. This is my command: Love each other."

John 15:9–17

chapter thirty-seven
· · · · ·
Compared to What?

I ran into a friend after her ladies' Bible study recently. She didn't look like a mom who had just enjoyed a refreshing tiptoe through God's Word. Actually, she looked a little more like she'd been through a minefield. How could a lady come out of Bible study looking so distressed? When I asked her about it, she said she went in a good mom and came out a bad one.

How Could That Happen?

Right off the bat one of the women had asked my friend when her son would be completely potty trained. Her son is eight months old. "Why, little Amanda potty trained herself by the time she was nine months old," the mom gushed. "That's when I knew I should send her to an advanced preschool. What preschool is Michael attending, dear? What? What do you mean, 'he's not'?"

Another mom in the group chimed in: "Well, I decided to home school. I couldn't find a preschool that offered graphic engineering. Of course, I've had to enlist a tutor for French. So how many languages does little Michael speak?"

Others jumped in:

"Jenny always obeys the first time—doesn't your child?"

"I think all preschoolers should do their own laundry like my Frankie."

"She was born with a head full of perfect blonde curls."

"He walked at six months."

"She did calculus at two."

My friend had walked in as the mom of a perfect, beautiful baby boy and come out a failing parent of a bald, toothless eight-month-old kid who didn't walk or do higher math and only knew one language. Okay, he didn't even know one language, but how could she admit it to those Wonder Moms? Somewhere in the minefield of comparison those explosive feelings of failure and defeat blasted her.

Observing vs. Comparing

We all can go a little ballistic now and then when it comes to comparing our kids to other kids and our parenting skills to those of other parents. There's a fine yet volatile line between observing and comparing. Observing is a great way to learn. Paul gave us his version of "Do what I say *and* what I do" in 1 Corinthians 11:1: "Follow my example, as I follow the example of Christ." It's great to watch godly examples, then evaluate and learn from them. But we head into the minefield when we stop learning and start comparing.

Comparing ourselves to others is a lose/lose proposition. We either measure a false sense of our own goodness and come out on the pride side, or we come away with an off-balance sense of our own shortcomings and end up feeling crushed. Comparing inspires jealousy, conceit, bitterness, arrogance, envy, defeat, and more.

Comparing our children to their siblings or to other children can be disastrous, too. We can find ourselves pouring bitterness into a daughter who never feels she measures up to her big sister. Or we can frustrate a son by trying to remake him into the kid down the block. Isn't it sad when we make our kids feel like failures because we're fighting feelings of failure as parents? Every now and then we need to ask ourselves, *Do I want my child to do well for his own benefit, or is my goal to look good as a parent?* When we find our focus is on our parenting more than on the well-being of our kids, it's time to put down the yardstick and stop the measuring madness.

Put Down the Yardstick and Slowly Step Away

What should you do when you feel you don't measure up? What should you do when you feel your kids aren't measuring up? It's really pretty simple: stop measuring.

Our kids don't become good kids by measuring up to someone else's expectations. And we don't become good parents by comparing to the group. We become good parents by loving our children unconditionally, instructing them, encouraging and disciplining them, admitting our own failures, asking for forgiveness, and, overall, lining up our parenting—and our lives—with the Word of God.

Second Corinthians 10:12 says, "When they measure themselves by themselves and compare themselves with themselves, they are not wise."

So let's be wise. Let's toss the stick and enjoy our kids—even if they still eat the crayons instead of using them for trig.

Doing a Stick Check

Have you ever caught yourself making someone else feel smaller in order to pump up your own ego? Are you ever guilty of pulling out the yardstick to prove someone else doesn't measure up?

Measuring isn't our job. Our job is to lighten others' loads, not heap on more junk. We're instructed not only to lighten the load, but to carry it! Galatians 6:2, 4 (HCSB) says, "Carry one another's burdens; in this way you will fulfill the law of Christ. ... But each person should examine his own work, and then he will have a reason for boasting in himself alone, and not in respect to someone else." We also find verse 4 phrased this way: "Each one should test his own actions. Then he can take pride in himself, without comparing himself to somebody else."

Sound like a better life? No comparison!

The world is unprincipled. It's dog-eat-dog out there! The world doesn't fight fair. But we don't live or fight our battles that way—never have and never will. The tools of our trade aren't for marketing or manipulation, but they are for demolishing that entire massively corrupt culture. We use our powerful God-tools for smashing warped philosophies, tearing down barriers erected against the truth of God, fitting every loose thought and emotion and impulse into the structure of life shaped by Christ. Our tools are ready at hand for clearing the ground of every obstruction and building lives of obedience into maturity....We're not, understand, putting ourselves in a league with those who boast that they're our superiors. We wouldn't dare do that. But in all this comparing and grading and competing, they quite miss the point.

2 Corinthians 10:1–6, 12, The Message

chapter thirty-eight
Flourish

Can I just admit that I'm not much on kid cereals? Not long ago I found myself in a breakfast pinch (meaning I was out of every other breakfast choice on the planet), and I poured myself a bowl of "their" cereal. One of the kids came along and said, "Ooh, I love that stuff!" That's almost always a sure sign I'd probably rather swallow dishwashing liquid.

One taste told me I was right. "This is disgusting," I said, trying not to let any more of the stuff touch my tongue before it went down. "I didn't just blow a bubble, did I?" In all fairness, it did leave a fruity scent in the bowl and a spot-free shine.

I didn't give up on kid breakfasts without first trying one of their toaster tarts. I tried to keep an open mind—really I did. But that first bite made me think I'd chomped into a no-pest strip. I checked the ingredients panel. Whew, no insecticides listed—not anything presently known to be insecticides anyway.

Snap, Crackle, Pop Quiz

Not only is there no love lost on kid breakfasts, I confess that I don't even completely understand them. Has anyone else wondered, for instance, why Cap'n

Crunch's eyebrows are totally disconnected from his head? They're hanging there in midair, dancing around a hat that's bigger than his body. Poor guy. Surely it's been thirty years or more that he's been in the cereal military, and he's not yet managed to get those eyebrows attached to his forehead.

All my life I've been a breakfast eater, and I still haven't answered those big breakfast questions. In addition to the eyebrow quandary, for instance, I can't tell you how long I've wondered why a rabbit can't eat kid cereal, how many different kinds of marshmallow charms they can add before the cereal is one big box of marshmallows, and if it's "all part of this nutritious breakfast," what do I do about the other part? And I don't know if it was just me, but I always thought that bird, Sonny, had already had one Cocoa Puff too many.

So maybe I haven't learned all the breakfast answers, but I have learned that I don't have to understand my kids' tastes in breakfast to love them. I adore my children with an enormous and enthusiastic love.

Soul Fruit

God's Word has so much to say about how we love. In Philippians 1:9–11 (MSG), Paul said, "So this is my prayer: that your love will flourish and that you will not only love much but well. Learn to love appropriately. You need to use your head and test your feelings so that your love is sincere and intelligent, not sentimental gush. Live a lover's life, circumspect and exemplary, a life Jesus will be proud of: bountiful in fruits from the soul, making Jesus Christ attractive to all, getting everyone involved in the glory and praise of God." The life of one who loves well is a life "bountiful in fruits from the soul." It's the perfect soul food!

Love with an eye roll? No, we're instructed not only

to love much, but to love "well." Should we be surprised when we run across another Christian who is difficult to love? I don't think our heavenly Father would've devoted so much of Scripture to instructions in relationships if they were always going to be cinchy. Don't be surprised, but surprise yourself as your love for challenging people flourishes beyond what you're able to do yourself. That flourish is evidence of the Holy Spirit working in your life, loving with his love.

Lovely Love

According to the Philippians passage, it's the fruit of living a life of love that will make Jesus attractive to others. Jesus said in John 13:35 (HCSB), "By this all people will know that you are My disciples, if you have love for one another."

We need to do a love evaluation from time to time and inspect our own fruit. Is the love we're showing attracting other people? Are we doing anything in the flesh that might repel others? Does our love get others involved in praising God?

The Most Important Meal of the Day

How do we learn to let our love flourish? How do we allow the Lord to get rid of the corrupt things and work out his kind of love in our lives? We can start by making sure his Word is an important part of our spiritual nutrition. It's our milk. First Peter 2:2–3 (HCSB) says, "Like newborn infants, desire the unadulterated spiritual milk, so that you may grow by it in [your] salvation, since you have tasted that the Lord is good."

Ever tried putting water on cereal? Talk about a "cereal" killer. We need the right milk to grow. We need to make sure we're starting every day in his Word—not just reading about his Word, but making sure we have a balanced Bible diet. It's the breakfast of champions— the way to nourish and flourish!

Flourish till the Finish

Philippians 1:6 (MSG) says, "There has never been the slightest doubt in my mind that the God who started this great work in you would keep at it and bring it to a flourishing finish on the very day Christ Jesus appears." I've noticed when we're allowing the Lord to love through us, he really does help us make him look good. That makes life sweet—sweeter than the sweetest toaster tart!

Incidentally, I've also noticed that since taking a bite of the toaster pop-up thing, I haven't once been bothered by flying insects.

So, chosen by God for this new life of love, dress in the wardrobe God picked out for you: compassion, kindness, humility, quiet strength, discipline. Be even-tempered, content with second place, quick to forgive an offense. Forgive as quickly and completely as the Master forgave you. And regardless of what else you put on, wear love. It's your basic, all-purpose garment. Never be without it. Let the peace of Christ keep you in tune with each other, in step with each other. None of this going off and doing your own thing. And cultivate thankfulness. Let the Word of Christ—the Message—have the run of the house. Give it plenty of room in your lives. Instruct and direct one another using good common sense. And sing, sing your hearts out to God! Let every detail in your lives—words, actions, whatever—be done in the name of the Master, Jesus, thanking God the Father every step of the way.

Colossians 3:12–17, THE MESSAGE

chapter thirty-nine
. . . . .
The Word on Words

For three days in a row I've had that "song that never ends" stuck in my head. *Oh Lord, give me grace.* My kids started singing it in the car last week. After awhile they tried to sing it as a round. That was so "not pretty" that it was hilarious—and just a little troubling. No, it was definitely not a round song.

It is, however, a lot like a computer virus. It entered my brain and has been interfering with my internal processing ever since. Imagine me in bed staring up at the ceiling with this silly song playing over and over again in my head. Somebody, make it stop.

Once an annoying song gets stuck in my brain, it seems to grow. The more I try to get it out, the more it grows roots and imbeds itself. My brain must be like fertilizer for irritating songs. If only I could sprinkle some of this gray matter on my garden! I'm not sure I like this comparison, but I think my brain might be better than manure. There's growth power in there somewhere!

It Only Takes a Spark

Words are powerful little rascals. The words to that blasted song, for instance, have had the power to make me just a tad crazy for three days. The words we say can also tear down or they can build up. They can spark great inspiration or spark heated arguments. James 3:5–6 (MSG) says, "A word out of your mouth may seem of no account, but it can accomplish nearly anything—or destroy it! It only takes a spark, remember, to set off a forest fire. A careless or wrongly placed word out of your mouth can do that."

When we give the Lord our hearts, our marriages, and our families, we need to make sure our words are part of the deal. How many relationships have been blown apart by explosive word fallout? The passage in James 3 continues: "By our speech we can ruin the world, turn harmony to chaos, throw mud on a reputation, send the whole world up in smoke and go up in smoke with it, smoke right from the pit of hell."

Word Whacker

Weed out the words you don't need like you would weed your garden. Well, actually, I hope we all do better at word-weeding than I do at keeping the weeds out of my flower beds. One way to weed out the fiery words is to cultivate words of grace. Graciousness leaves little room for those mud-slinging, anger-sparking words. Colossians 4:6 (MSG) says, "Be gracious in your speech. The goal is to bring out the best in others in a conversation, not put them down, not cut them out."

When we're focusing on others in our conversations, desiring what's best for them, we're not only cultivating words of grace, but we're also setting loving, gracious examples for our children to follow. And need I even mention that we're setting examples when we use unkind words, too? Harsh, disrespectful, abrasive words spoken to our children will come back to haunt us. Titus 2:7–8 (TLB) says, "And here you yourself must be an example to them of good deeds of every kind. Let everything you do reflect your love of the truth and the fact that you are in dead earnest about it. Your conversation should be so sensible and logical that anyone who wants to argue will be ashamed of himself because there won't be anything to criticize in anything you say!"

Our words need to reflect goodness, kindness, love, truth, and sincerity. They should be sensible and logical when we're sharing the truths of Christ. When we use these kinds of words, we become the good examples to our children that we want to be. These words are also an example and a blessing to our spouses, our own parents, our friends—everyone we meet.

Word Power

Words really are powerful. Let's use the power for good. Remember that words are catchy, too. People will hear your words and repeat them. And they'll continue saying them forever just because ... *aw, man!*

We all stumble in many ways. If anyone is never at fault in what he says, he is a perfect man, able to keep his whole body in check. When we put bits into the mouths of horses to make them obey us, we can turn the whole animal. Or take ships as an example. Although they are so large and are driven by strong winds, they are steered by a very small rudder wherever the pilot wants to go. Likewise the tongue is a small part of the body, but it makes great boasts. Consider what a great forest is set on fire by a small spark. The tongue also is a fire, a world of evil among the parts of the body. It corrupts the whole person, sets the whole course of his life on fire, and is itself set on fire by hell. All kinds of animals, birds, reptiles and creatures of the sea are being tamed and have been tamed by man, but no man can tame the tongue.

It is a restless evil, full of deadly poison. With the tongue we praise our Lord and Father, and with it we curse men, who have been made in God's likeness. Out of the same mouth come praise and cursing. My brothers, this should not be. Can both fresh water and salt water flow from the same spring? My brothers, can a fig tree bear olives, or a grapevine bear figs? Neither can a salt spring produce fresh water. Who is wise and understanding among you? Let him show it by his good life, by deeds done in the humility that comes from wisdom. But if you harbor bitter envy and selfish ambition in your hearts, do not boast about it or deny the truth. Such "wisdom" does not come down from heaven but is earthly, unspiritual, of the devil. For where you have envy and self-ish ambition, there you find disorder and every evil practice. But the wisdom that comes from heaven is first of all pure; then peace-loving, considerate, submissive, full of mercy and good fruit, impartial and sincere. Peacemakers who sow in peace raise a harvest of righteousness.

James 3:2–18

chapter forty

. . . . .

Let Us Spray

You wouldn't believe the amount of hairspray one household of seven people goes through in a week. Imagine seven heads of unruly hair. We have light hold, extra hold, extra-extra hold, extra-ridiculously-stiff-like-your-favorite-whisk-broom hold, and, my favorite, polyurethane. I've been told that we should stay in well-ventilated areas when we do hair. And we should never coif near an open flame.

You might be glad to know that I buy all those varieties of hairspray in pump bottles—mostly because I worry that if we were an aerosol family, there'd be a hole in the ozone layer right over our house.

You might be interested to know that there are several members of my family who can jump on the trampoline without their hair ever moving. When the wind blows, the hair all blows up in one piece. I've wondered if we should install hinges so we don't have to worry about a big hair flap snapping off. I think I actually felt my feet leave the ground on one extra windy day. It's *The Flying Nun* revisited—and without the hat. We give the term "hat hair" a whole new meaning.

When Andrew was younger, he used to use the plastered hair flap on the top as a spitball springboard. He said it made a great slingshot. He lost many a spitball in that hair, though. Once I noticed two of them stuck up there. They looked just like little eyeballs on top of his head. Boy was it creepy to look at his hair and have it look back. He thought it was funny. I'm sure if he'd thought of it, he would've gibed, "Hair's looking at you!"

The Family That Sprays Together...

At least I don't have to worry about us sticking together as a family. If I ever see us drifting apart, all I'll have to do is sneak up behind everyone and press all our heads together. If we're not "chummy," we can at least be "gummy."

Sticking together as a family really has become so much easier—all hairdo's aside—since all of my kids have become followers of Christ. It's become so much more pleasant, too. I wonder if there's anything in life that brings joy to parents like seeing our children come to a place where they understand their need for a savior and decide to give their hearts and lives to Christ.

All of us have a need for a savior. Since sin entered the world in the Garden of Eden, we've all been separated from a holy God. Every one of us since Adam and Eve has sinned. Romans 3:10–11 says, "There is no one righteous, not even one; there is no one who understands, no one who seeks God."

But God loves us in the most powerfully surprising, "hair-raising" way. Even though we were unlovable, Jesus came as part of God's gracious love plan. "But God demonstrates his own love for us in this: While we were still sinners, Christ died for us" Romans 5:8 says. Jesus lived a sinless life and died a sacrificial death on the cross to pay our sin penalty. Romans 3:23–25 says, "For all have sinned and fall short of the glory of God, and are justified freely by his grace through the redemption that came by Christ Jesus. God presented him as a sacrifice of atonement, through faith in his blood."

New Life

When he died on the cross, Jesus took the punishment for every sin you've ever committed—past, present, and future. Once you've accepted Christ, you're declared righteous in the eyes of God. Romans 3:22 says, "This righteousness from God comes through faith in Jesus Christ to all who believe." Three days after Jesus died, he rose from the dead, conquering sin and death once and for all. He's alive! And when we ask him to forgive our sin and to come into our lives and take control, he does just that. We can believe the promise of Romans 10:13: "Everyone who calls on the name of the Lord will be saved."

When we give him our lives, he makes us new. His unconditional, selfless, sacrificial, extravagant love has made new life—eternal life—possible for all who will receive him. Ephesians 1:5–11 (MSG) spells it out so beautifully.

> Long, long ago he decided to adopt us into his family through Jesus Christ. (What pleasure he took in planning this!) He wanted us to enter into the celebration of his lavish gift-giving by the hand of his beloved Son. Because of the sacrifice of the Messiah, his blood poured out on the altar of the Cross, we're a free people—free of penalties and punishments chalked up by all our misdeeds. And not just barely free, either. Abundantly free! He thought of everything, provided for everything we could possibly need, letting us in on the plans he took such delight in making. He set it all out before us in Christ, a

long-range plan in which everything would be brought together and summed up in him, everything in deepest heaven, everything on planet earth. It's in Christ that we find out who we are and what we are living for.

Would You Like to Become Part of His Family?

If you've been wondering what you're living for, take a good look at the plan your Maker has graciously formulated for you. Wouldn't it be great to live in the "abundant" freedom that passage talks about? If you've never responded to God's love-plan for you, you can. Even now. It doesn't matter where you are or what you're doing—even what hairstyle you're sporting. If you've never given your life to Christ, this could be the moment that changes your eternal destiny. If you haven't yet surrendered your life to him, I'm convinced it's no accident that God has brought you to this place—or to this page.

Would you like to get in on the abundant, forever life? Let Jesus know about it. You can pray something like this:

Lord, I know I've sinned. Would you please forgive me? I believe you died on the cross to pay for everything I've ever done wrong. I believe you rose again, victorious over sin and death. I trust you right now to give me a clean slate—to forgive every sin. Thank you for forgiving me and for loving me so overwhelmingly. Thank you for treasuring me as someone worthwhile—even as someone precious. I give you my life and my all. I pray you'll help me to become more and more like Jesus and that you'll use me in whatever way you want to bring glory to yourself for all the rest of my life. Thank you for saving me. In Jesus' name, Amen.

If you just prayed this kind of prayer for the first time, your life has been radically and eternally changed. All the sin that had gummed up your life is forever gone! You've been given a new life!

Let someone know what's going on in your life. Let a solid believer help you as you get started in your new walk with Christ. And let me be the first to welcome you into the family! It's the family of God! And it's the kind of family that will stick with you forever—even without radical hair chemicals. Don't worry—it's completely nonflammable, too!

The Family's Real Union

Surrendering your life to Christ brings a new and amazing love into your family. His Holy Spirit will be working in your life, teaching you about his glorious, extravagant love. This is the kind of surrender that can transform your entire family. Remember the passage in Ephesians 5:1–4 (MSG) we looked at in the very first chapter? "Watch what God does, and then you do it, like children who learn proper behavior from their parents. Mostly what God does is love you. Keep company with him and learn a life of love. Observe how Christ loved us. His love was not cautious but extravagant. He didn't love in order to get something from us but to give everything of himself to us. Love like that." Just watch—his sweeping love may just transform your entire family!

Even if we never meet this side of heaven, I find such joy in knowing we'll meet in the eternal place he's preparing for us. We're family. Isn't it fun to think about how everything will be absolutely perfect in that sin-free environment?

One day, our feet really will leave the ground. We'll begin a wondrous eternity together. Look for me, will you? I'll be the one with the perfect, yet spray-free hair.

See you at the family reunion!

But in our time something new has been added. What Moses and the prophets witnessed to all those years has happened. The God-setting-things-right that we read about has become Jesus-setting-things-right for us. And not only for us, but for everyone who believes in him. For there is no difference between us and them in this. Since we've compiled this long and sorry record as sinners (both us and them) and proved that we are utterly incapable of living the glorious lives God wills for us, God did it for us. Out of sheer generosity he put us in right standing with himself. A pure gift. He got us out of the mess we're in and restored us to where he always wanted us to be. And he did it by means of Jesus Christ.

God sacrificed Jesus on the altar of the world to clear that world of sin. Having faith in him sets us in the clear. God decided on this course of action in full view of the public— to set the world in the clear with himself through the sacrifice of Jesus, finally taking care of the sins he had so patiently endured. This is not only clear, but it's now—this is current history! God sets things right. He also makes it possible for us to live in his rightness.

Romans 3:21–26, THE MESSAGE

notes

· · · · ·

Chapter 1
1. Dr. James C. Dobson, *Complete Marriage and Family Home Reference Guide* (Wheaton, Ill.: Tyndale, 2000), 166.

Chapter 6
1. Dr. James C. Dobson, *Parenting Isn't for Cowards* (Nashville: Word, 1987), 121.

Chapter 14
1. Dr. James C. Dobson, *Love for a Lifetime* (Sisters, Ore.: Multnomah, 2003), 65.

Chapter 16
1. Dr. James C. Dobson, *Complete Marriage and Family Home Reference Guide* (Wheaton, Ill.: Tyndale, 2000), 167.

Chapter 34
1. Rick Warren, *The Purpose-Driven® Life* (Grand Rapids, Mich.: Zondervan, 2002), 79.

Readers' Guide

For Personal Reflection
or Group Discussion

Serving Up Hope and Hilarity Family Style

Every once in awhile I have to ask myself if I'm really willing to completely give all—to sacrifice my comfort, my warmth, whatever I might be tempted to hang on to."

After all, the cat did when she ended up in the refrigerator, a place where the sacrifice was great, but so was the reward of food. Rhonda Rhea challenges us to consider what we hold on to and how it affects the core of who our family can be.

Without a doubt, one of the most rewarding and challenging places for us to live out our relationship with Christ is at home. But there is no place more important for our children to learn about who Christ is and to find that they, too, desire a relationship with him. "Families are eternally more important than main dishes or bicycles."

As Deuteronomy 6:7–9 says, "Impress them on your children. Talk about them when you sit at home and when you walk along the road, when you lie down and when you get up. Tie them as symbols on your hands and bind them on your foreheads. Write them on the doorframes of your houses and on your gates." We want our children to see Christ in our lives, but in observations that only Rhonda can share, we know that discipling comes with laughter, accidents, messes, and love.

"God's Word is something we never want to leave on the

back burner. It's the manual that equips us in even the most strenuous bicycle-building moments and helps us make every part of family life a 'good work.'" As we laugh about, remember, and share those "experiences" that happen in our family and with others, the need for constant connection with Christ will become clearer.

The intent of the following study guide, and indeed this entire book, is to support and inspire you to dig even more deeply into God's Word as you relate to your family on a daily, consistent basis. "Get ready to STOP the busyness for a minute or two, DROP to your knees when the Lord calls you to, and ROLL on the floor laughing when you need to!"

The questions have been designed for use by individuals or groups. Use this guide during your personal devotions, with a prayer partner, in a Bible study group, or a Sunday school class. However you utilize this study, may you gain a deeper understanding of the love and dreams you have for your family as well as have a few laughs to make the adventure more fun.

Part I: Rip–Roaring Recipes for Fast–moving Fun—Relying on Christ in the Adventure

Chapter One: Watch Me!

1. Think about a time recently when you were "watching God." What did you see him do in your life?

2. Colossians 4:2 tells us to be "watchful and thankful." What are some areas in your life where you need to watch for God and imitate him?

3. As your kids watch you, how can you help them see more about who God is in your daily routine?

Chapter Two: Who's Your Provider?

1. Think about your own situation right now. What are some ways that God has provided for your material needs today?

2. Sometimes it's easy to see the material things that God has provided. But how has he provided for you spiritually recently?

3. Psalm 145:3–8 says, "Great is the LORD and most worthy of praise; his greatness no one can fathom." Take some time to praise him for providing for you and your family.

Chapter Three: Space Invaders

1. We all get overwhelmed as parents at one time or another. What are some times that you find you need "space"?

2. Sometimes all we need is fifteen minutes away from the situation to revitalize ourselves. How can you find time to spend alone with the Lord?

3. Rhonda talks about how the disciples were surprised after what they thought was going to be a getaway turned out to be a dinner for five thousand people. What are some unexpected situations that you have experienced?

4. As you consider the Seven Keepers that Rhonda suggests to save space, which one do you need to make your highest priority? What do you need to do to make this happen?

Chapter Four: What's in a Name?

1. Many people have a story that goes with how their name was chosen. How did your parents decide on your name? Is there a legacy that goes with your name?

2. Of course, the best thing about our name is that it can be attached to "child of God." What does it mean to you that you are a child of God?

3. In Philippians 2:1–11, Paul gave us a description of Christ and his attitude toward what God had sent him to earth to accomplish. How can you relate this passage to your own call to "grow up" your family? What areas will you focus on?

Chapter Five: Hope on a Rope

1. Our children have those times when they cannot seem to stay with us no matter how we beg or yell. Share a time you needed to put your children on a rope tied to you.

2. Rhonda says that "sometimes coming to the end of our rope means coming to the end of ourselves." What does she mean by that? Why is it so difficult?

3. To find "hope on a rope," we need to strip away our pride and get out of God's way. How can you allow God to lead you in your area of self-sufficiency?

Part 2: A Dash of This, a Dash of That——

Dealing with the Busyness of Life

Chapter Six: Help, I Need a Clone!

1. If you had a clone, what would you need her to do for you today?

2. Rhonda gives several suggestions on how to get organized. How about you? What can you do to be more organized at home? At work?

3. Since there isn't a 1-800-GRAN-AID number, who is a "grandma" you could call for help?

4. "Sometimes you can find relief by getting a new take." Which "New Take" do you need most right now?

5. Relate a "laugh" you have experienced with your children lately. How can you find more of these moments to "double your blessings"?

Chapter Seven: Just a Closer Sprint with Thee

1. "It's easy to let the family activity level get out of hand." What are some signs at your house that you need to tweak your schedule?

2. Luke 1:68–79 tells us about our need for peace. How can you be more in tune with the "path of peace" and "living inner stillness"?

3. Though it is difficult to have peace when we are sprinting with our children from one place to another or trying to keep up with the challenges of our home, we can. What are some characteristics of a parent who "rests in the peace of God"? How can you have more of these characteristics in your life?

Chapter Eight: Hope for the Housework Impaired

1. All of our homes can get "out-of-control" on occasion. What contributes to your home getting out-of-control? How do you respond when you feel your home is in this condition?

2. Rhonda tells us to "focus on Christ and everything else will fall into line." What does this focusing involve, and how will you know if you are focused?

3. Paul had a "passionate enthusiasm in regard to doing what he perceived to be the work of God." How can you decide what really needs to be done in your home?

Chapter Nine: The Juggling Act

1. Tending to get caught up in all the stresses of family, we try to juggle everything that we have on our calendars. What are the things that you are juggling with your family?

2. Rhonda suggests some tips for handling all we try to juggle. Which juggling tip do you need to work on most? What can you do today (this week) to make this tip work for you?

3. Psalm 127:1 states, "Unless the LORD builds the house, its builders labor in vain." Have you committed your home to the Lord as general contractor? How can you make his leadership a part of your work at home?

Chapter Ten: Running in Place vs. Stepping in Grace

1. Rhonda talks about how we exchange our time for many things. How do you "spend" your time?

2. "Time spent on the foolishness of sin has no place in a life of grace." What busyness do you need to exchange for a more fruitful life?

3. In Ephesians 5:8–12 we read, "You groped your way through that murk once, but no longer. You're out in the open now. The bright light of Christ makes your way plain. So no more stumbling around. Get on with it! The good, the right, the true—these are the actions appropriate for daylight hours. Figure out what will please Christ, and then do it." Even in the busiest times, God can be in control. How can you find more grace in the moments of your day, especially for yourself?

Part 3: Blend Together Thoroughly——Keeping Christ at the Center of Every Relationship

Chapter Eleven: Lord of My Rings

1. According to Rhonda, what is a covenant? How can recognizing that marriage is based on a covenant help hold it together?

2. Read Philippians 2:3–8. What are some of the characteristics of a strong marriage?

3. "Our marriage is the strongest at those times when we're careful not to misplace the most important issue—our spiritual connection in Christ." How can you avoid misplacing your spiritual connection to Christ? How does this strengthen a marriage?

Chapter Twelve: Marriage . . . and Other Great Experiments

1. The first mysterious marriage experiment was in Genesis 2:23–24. How would you describe your "marriage experiment"? What has God taught you through being married to your spouse?

2. Rhonda suggests an equation that will equal a successful marriage. How do you rate yourself in this equation? What do you need to submit to Jesus to make it work?

3. How can a marriage relationship be a mirror of God's grace to others?

Chapter Thirteen: Every Single Time

1. "A family who is surviving divorce is certainly no less a family. The Lord can hold, even bind, families together as

they rely on him." How can you come alongside a single parent to help her keep her family strong?

2. Say a friend of yours comes to you struggling with a mistake he or she has made or a mistake someone else has made. What would you say to your friend to help him see past the mistake and to believe God has a plan?

3. Share a time that you "let Jesus carry you." What was the result?

Chapter Fourteen: Men Are Computers, Women Are Cell Phones

1. Rhonda compares men to computers and women to cell phones. When have you seen these similarities in yourself or in your spouse?

2. Which strategy that Rhonda suggests do you need to use to become better "connected" with your spouse?

3. What does "checking your server" involve? How can checking your server help you build your relationship stronger and deeper in Christ?

Chapter Fifteen: Say Cheese

1. What are some ways you can develop a friendship? What kinds of activities would you choose to develop more thoroughly?

2. Who is your best friend? Describe her and what it is that makes you close friends.

3. Rhonda suggests three ways that developing good conversation skills will help build better friendships. Which one would you start with to develop your conversation skills?

4. Do you have a friend you need to forgive without reservation? Commit to forgiving him or her today.

Part 4: Sticking to the Recipe, Tasting Sweet Results—Disciplining and Instructing

Chapter Sixteen: Not Just Another Pretty Plate

1. Share a time that your children "caught" you reading God's Word. What was their reaction? What was your reaction?

2. It's important to be consistent with family devotion time, but what is the key to making devotions meaningful to children? How can you incorporate this into your time with your children?

3. In what other ways can you make sure that family devotion time is meaningful for children?

Chapter Seventeen: Filtered

1. "God's Word protects our families spiritually." How does God's Word act as our "sin filter"? How does God use his Word to filter out those things that don't glorify him?

2. Relate a time that you needed to "head straight for God's Word." How did God use his Word to change your perspective on a situation, to change your attitude, or to lead you in how you should handle a situation?

3. For you to walk in God's Word as it is described in Psalm 119, what changes do you need to make in your own life?

Chapter Eighteen: Contentment Under Construction

1. Some may say that you would have to look for a long while to find someone who is content with what she has. What are the challenges to being content in our culture?

2. How would you rate your children in terms of their contentment?

3. Rhonda makes suggestions about "constructing" contentment in our children. Which one would you begin with in your children? What other ideas do you have to teach your children to be content?

4. After taking the contentment quiz, what areas do you personally need to work on? What steps can you take to be more content with what God has given you?

Chapter Nineteen: Well-grounded Kids

1. What are some discipline choices you have made with your child that have been successful? What are some that didn't work well?

2. "Most kids are incredibly skilled at finding our anger triggers—then they yank them for all they're worth." How can you determine if anger is guiding your discipline with a child?

3. "Hurting our children in anger doesn't bring about a change of heart in a child." What are some strategies for stepping away from a situation in which you find yourself responding in anger?

4. Using Rhonda's "Rules on Rules," give examples of how you can lead your children to be well grounded.

Chapter Twenty: Shod Those Tiny Feet

1. What experiences have you had with a family devotional time? Do you have any experiences or preconceptions that might keep you from having devotions in your home?

2. Our kids can behave all kinds of ways when we are trying to share a family devotional time. What is the most challenging thing about having a family devotion time in your home?

3. "We need to remember that, as important as our family devotion time is, the way we live our lives the rest of the day will teach our children more." How can you be more effective in the devotional time you spend with your family? What are some areas you need to address personally to be more effective with your children?

Part 5: If at First You Don't Succeed, Fry, Fry Again—Persevering through the Challenging Moments

Chapter Twenty-one: Driving Ms. Rhonda

1. "Raising kids is a series of instances of letting go." What decisions might you let go of and allow your children to make this week?

2. Why do you think that giving up control to our children is so challenging?

3. "We need to keep on trusting Jesus to get us through the sometimes painful experiences of letting go." What do you need to do to trust God's work in the lives of your children?

Chapter Twenty-two: Band-aid Stickers and Scrapbook Moments

1. "Physical difficulties, emotional challenges, disappointments from family members—bad things can happen to good families." Why is it difficult to trust God when we're hurting?

2. Share a time where you experienced God caring for you in the midst of a struggle. What did you learn about God?

3. If you are experiencing a struggle now, commit yourself anew to lean and rely on Christ and to stay in God's Word.

Chapter Twenty-three: When the Going Gets Tough, the Tough Get Pinging

1. Rhonda talks about her own "tests" at the dentist. Share an experience that you have had at one of your own testing places.

2. God leads us all through trials and tests. What is a test you have gone through where you came "forth as gold"?

3. "It's tough to go through a test without whining." How can you "shine" through your present or future test? How can you avoid whining?

Chapter Twenty-four: Hope Springs Eternal

1. Share one of your "impossible, demanding, draining, soda-exploding days." How did you find God's hope in the midst of the situation? What did you learn that made dealing with the next impossible day easier?

2. "Hope is a shield over our hearts and minds that keeps us looking at the important things in life—eternal things." What is hope to you? How can you hold on to hope in every challenge?

3. "To you, O LORD, I lift up my soul; in you I trust, O my God. Do not let me be put to shame, nor let my enemies triumph over me. No one whose hope is in you will ever be put to shame, but they will be put to shame who are treacherous without excuse. Show me your ways, O LORD, teach me your paths; guide me in your truth and teach me, for you are God my Savior, and my hope is in you all day long" (Psalm 25:1–5). What direction does Psalm 25:1–5 give for a situation in which you need hope right now? How will you follow these guidelines in the midst of what is going on in your life?

Chapter Twenty-five: Learning to Let Go

1. Talk about a time that you let go of your child or something in his or her life in a very tangible way.

2. After reading the lyrics of Rhonda's song about letting go, what do you find that challenges you in letting go of your children? What is God teaching you about letting go of your children?

3. "A mother is not a person to lean on, but a person to make leaning unnecessary." What does it mean to be a person who makes leaning unnecessary? How can you be a mother who provides this lesson to her children?

Part 6: Stirring up a Big Batch of Belief—Building Family Faith

Chapter Twenty-six: No Grain, No Gain

1. In your own words, define *faith*.

2. "Without understanding our heavenly Father, our faith is small and we live in fear." How is faith a part of your life? How can you build faith into your daily routine?

3. Hebrews 11 lists people in the Bible whose faith is legendary: Noah, Abraham, Isaac, Jacob, and others. Share a time when your faith was "legendary," a time when believing in him helped you see God at work in your life and/or the lives of others.

Chapter Twenty-seven: Ready or Not——Here He Comes

1. We all have had an unexpected guest at the door. Relate a time that you were caught off guard and not ready for company.

2. "First John 2:28 (MSG) indicates there will be those who are caught off guard in the most embarrassing moment of all time. 'Live deeply in Christ. Then we'll be ready for him when he appears, ready to receive him with open arms, with no cause for red-faced guilt or lame excuses when he

arrives.'" Rate yourself on how ready you are for Christ. What can you do to be caught "living deeply"?

3. How can living as if Christ is coming change the way you approach your day? What do you need to do differently to show that you are expecting company—Jesus Christ?

Chapter Twenty-eight: Living Large

1. "As we live in his big love, we learn that we can trust him in the biggest way." When has God surprised you with how "big" his grace is?

2. If our part, according to Isaiah 55:6–7 and Psalm 86:5, is to "seek" and "call on the LORD," how can we do this on a daily basis?

3. "God forgives big. He loves big. He is big. And he gives us life in the biggest way. It's a turbocharged life with every option added in." If you live with this "big" perspective, how will your view of family change? Your view of God?

Chapter Twenty-nine: Mount Launder-more

1. Laundry is just one job in our homes that seems never-ending. What are some of the chores in your home that overwhelm you? What are your strategies for dealing with these tasks?

3. Share a time your children or your spouse surprised you by serving.

Chapter Thirty-three: Kid Threats

1. When has "God called you by your first, middle, and last name"? What did he call you to do? What challenges did you experience? What joys?

2. "Hebrews 6:10–12 tells us God notices when we keep on serving." Where are you serving faithfully? What keeps you going?

3. "Not only will we become more mature—it will happen right out there for everyone to see! Keep in mind what an impact your service will have on your life, your family, and on all those around you." How has serving helped you mature in your relationship with God?

Chapter Thirty-four: Who Put the Cat in the Refrigerator?

1. Though he could demand our all, God chooses to ask us to offer our all. How does God receive us when we offer ourselves to him?

2. What kinds of things are easy to hang on to when we go to God to offer ourselves?

3. According to Rick Warren in *The Purpose Driven Life®*, "God is not a cruel slave driver or bully." What is he then? How does he work in your life?

4. What are the ramifications of being "God's friend"? How can we be his friend?

Chapter Thirty-five: King of the Jungle

1. How do you show hospitality to others?

2. "The bottom line is that Jesus needs to be the King of all." If we offer hospitality to others, how are we showing them that Jesus is King? What do we show them about him?

3. Rhonda says she wants her "kids to learn to hold their things loosely and in a non-grumbly fashion." How can you teach your children to become "unselfish givers"?

2. Rhonda says that "one way to weed out fiery words is to cultivate words of grace." What are examples of "words of grace" you can use with your children?

3. How have your words affected your children, for both the positive and the negative? What do you want your words to reflect to them? Prayerfully consider how to consistently achieve the results you are looking for.

Chapter Forty: Let Us Spray

1. If you are a new Christian, share your decision to follow Christ with at least one other person. If you have been a Christian for a long time, think back to the circumstances surrounding your decision. Who helped you see your need for Christ? When did it happen? How?

2. "All of us have a need for a savior." How has knowing Christ impacted you, your family, and your world?

3. After working through the devotions in this book, what changes do you think you need to make to show Christ to your family?

The Word at Work Around the World

A vital part of Cook Communications Ministries is our international outreach, Cook Communications Ministries International (CCMI). Your purchase of this book, and of other books and Christian-growth products from Cook, enables CCMI to provide Bibles and Christian literature to people in more than 150 languages in 65 countries.

Cook Communications Ministries is a not-for-profit, self-supporting organization. Revenues from sales of our books, Bible curricula, and other church and home products not only fund our U.S. ministry, but also fund our CCMI ministry around the world. One hundred percent of donations to CCMI go to our international literature programs.

CCMI reaches out internationally in three ways:

• Our premier International Christian Publishing Institute (ICPI) trains leaders from nationally led publishing houses around the world.

• We provide literature for pastors, evangelists, and Christian workers in their national language.

• We reach people at risk—refugees, AIDS victims, street children, and famine victims—with God's Word.

Word Power, God's Power

Faith Kidz, RiverOak, Honor, Life Journey, Victor, NexGen — every time you purchase a book produced by Cook Communications Ministries, you not only meet a vital personal need in your life or in the life of someone you love, but you're also a part of ministering to José in Colombia, Humberto in Chile, Gousa in India, or Lidiane in Brazil. You help make it possible for a pastor in China, a child in Peru, or a mother in West Africa to enjoy a life-changing book. And because you helped, children and adults around the world are learning God's Word and walking in his ways.

Thank you for your partnership in helping to disciple the world. May God bless you with the power of his Word in your life.

For more information about our international ministries, visit www.ccmi.org.

Additional copies of *WHO PUT THE CAT IN THE FRIDGE?*
are available from your local bookseller.

• • • • •

If you have enjoyed this book,
or if it has had an impact on your life,
we would like to hear from you.

Please contact us at:

LIFE JOURNEY
Cook Communications Ministries, Dept. 201
4050 Lee Vance View
Colorado Springs, CO 80918

Or at our Web site: www.cookministries.com

Bringing Home the Message for Life